TIME OUT

TIME OUT

*A teacher's year of reading,
fighting, and four-letter words*

LIANE SHAW

Second Story Press

Library and Archives Canada Cataloguing in Publication

Shaw, Liane, 1959–, author
Time out : a teacher's year of reading, fighting, and four-letter words /
by Liane Shaw.

Issued in print and electronic formats.
ISBN 978-1-927583-32-6 (pbk.). —ISBN 978-1-927583-33-3 (epub)

1. Shaw, Liane, 1959–. 2. Problem children—Education—Canada.
3. Mentally ill children—Education—Canada. 4. Teachers—Canada—
Biography. 5. Authors, Canadian (English)—21st century—Biography.
I. Title.

LA2325.S477A3 2014   371.10092   C2014-900020-0

C2014-900021-9

Edited by Carolyn Jackson
Copyedited by Kathryn White
Designed by Melissa Kaita

Cover photo © iStockphoto

Printed and bound in Canada

*Second Story Press gratefully acknowledges the support of the
Ontario Arts Council and the Canada Council for the Arts for our
publishing program. We acknowledge the financial support of the
Government of Canada through the Canada Book Fund.*

ONTARIO ARTS COUNCIL
CONSEIL DES ARTS DE L'ONTARIO
50 YEARS OF ONTARIO GOVERNMENT SUPPORT OF THE ARTS
50 ANS DE SOUTIEN DU GOUVERNEMENT DE L'ONTARIO AUX ARTS

Canada Council   Conseil des Arts
for the Arts   du Canada

MIX
Paper from
responsible sources
FSC
www.fsc.org   FSC® C004071

Published by
Second Story Press
20 Maud Street, Suite 401
Toronto, ON M5V 2M5
www.secondstorypress.ca

For David,
who taught me to look for the
gift inside of the moment.

INTRODUCTION

Before the beginning

Early on in my teaching career, I was presented with the amazing, albeit terrifying, opportunity to work with a group of "behavior kids"—children who had managed to outstay their welcomes in numerous elementary school classrooms. Overwhelmed with life and underwhelmed with support, these students took everything that came their way as a challenge to a fight.

Including me.

Maybe especially me!

For the next several years, I dealt with a steady stream of students whose lives were desperately out of control. The children came from all kinds of backgrounds: two parents, one parent, working parents, parents on welfare, foster parents, group homes. We had it all.

The one thing they had in common was that the efforts of the myriad of adults involved in their lives—parents, teachers, social workers, psychologists, doctors, even lawyers—never seemed to be quite enough to address the serious nature of their mental health issues. Too many schools, too many foster homes, not enough social workers, limited psychiatric hospital resources, lack of appropriate residential placements—the list went on and on.

It was an incredible journey, and as I traveled down the strange pathways that led to the lives of my students, I ended up learning far more than I taught. In later years, I often thought I would like to share some of our experiences in a book. I hesitated though, worried that perhaps readers would find it outdated. After all, it happened a long time ago.

Ten years after saying good-bye to my last group of "behavior kids," I took on the new challenge of working as a consultant for our school board. In this role, I once again came into regular contact with students with serious behavioral challenges and the teachers trying to work with them. And I discovered that very little had changed. There were still far too many students in need and far too few practical resources to provide long-term, sustainable support.

And so I decided to make an attempt at telling our story after all, or at least the first chapter. Names have been altered, locations changed, chronologies shifted, and the gender of the occasional adult switched to protect privacy. But the events are real. The children are real. And the issues are all too real.

Anyone who reads the daily news is aware that the mental health crisis facing our young people is still significant and is growing. But as awareness also grows, perhaps we will finally find a way to ensure that fifteen years from now—hopefully sooner—this story will finally be outdated.

CHAPTER 1

In the beginning

"I said sit down. Now!"

The teacher's voice is panicky instead of authoritative. They'll sniff it out like ponies, rearing up and throwing him off before he knows what happened.

"And I said fuck off. Now!"

The child's voice is authoritative instead of panicky. A resounding crash shakes the thin wall separating us. I think the teacher's down for the count.

I should do something, but I've been told not to interfere without an invitation. I don't hear anyone inviting me in.

I do hear laughter, high pitched and triumphant, accompanied by the sounds of running feet and objects being thrown. I have a sudden mental image of wild horses running across a farmer's field, hooves pounding out a path of destruction as they celebrate their freedom.

My grade seven Resource kids look at each other, eyes grinning, mouths carefully still so I won't notice. These are kids with learning issues who are struggling in class. They come to my room every day so I can help them figure out a way to access the math curriculum, although recently they've been a lot more interested in the vocabulary lessons coming from the other half of the room. I keep teaching, raising my voice to drown out the mayhem until I'm shouting out the virtues of Pythagoras for the whole school to hear.

The noise next door escalates until I can't ignore it anymore.

"Okay, I'm going to send you back to your classes a bit early today. Do what you can with this on your own, and we'll pick up the pieces tomorrow."

They pack up their books, grinning openly now. I'm pretty sure not one of them is going to be finishing up on their own. They all saunter down the hall, prolonging the brief moment of freedom.

I walk down to the neighboring door, wondering where the troops are. It's obvious there's a free-for-all going on here. Surely Peter's called the office by now.

The door opens suddenly, and he stumbles out into the hall. He leans against the wall and shakes his head. "I'm done. I can't do it anymore. I'm out of here. I called the office. Someone should be here soon."

Before I can say anything, he's gone. I look up and down the empty hallway. No troops. Just me.

I step to the door of his room and look in.

"Hey!" I raise my voice so that they can hear me, but since they're pretty busy throwing textbooks around and knocking over chairs, they don't notice me right away.

I watch them for a moment. It's kind of fascinating, really. The little blond in the corner is very methodical and careful, picking up each book and ripping every page out individually. The tall, dark-haired one with the wild eyes is much angrier. He tries to rip the whole book in half, getting more and more frustrated until he throws it across the room.

"Excuse me, please." I'm snapped out of my fascination by a hand on my arm. The principal and vice principal both scoot in past me to save the day.

The boys take one look at them and make like frustrated soccer stars, kicking at anything in their path as they run around the room. It's amazing how big a mess two little kids can make. I have to put my hand over my mouth to stop from laughing as Mrs. Callahan and Ms. Kruger run around after them, trying to get them to stop moving.

Two against two. The odds are not in the adults' favor.

"What's going on?" The voice in my ear startles me, and I whip around, hand still pressed against my mouth.

"I think Mrs. Callahan is teaching gym." An odd hiccupping noise escapes me as I try not to laugh. The man standing in front of me is straight from the board office. He's Mr. Norton, the consultant they send in to help us figure out what's going on with our kids and to act as a liaison with parents and staff and whoever else is involved in the overly complicated lives of students with special needs. Or is it students with special challenges? The politically correct rhetoric changes yearly. Whatever we call them, he helps me help them. And I probably should try to look professional in front of him. But it's really hard to do that when two babes in skirts and heels are running around chasing two kids in running shoes—two very agile kids in running shoes. The little blond one just shimmied his way up the bookshelf more efficiently than a spider monkey. I shake my head, accidentally grinning.

"Very talented," Mr. Norton says. He has a first name, but I can never remember it.

"Who? The kid or the administrator?"

"The kid, obviously. Never been a big fan of administrators," says the man from the board office.

"Oh, look, the other one is up there too!" I interrupt myself mid-sentence, not even trying to hide my laughter as the tall boy takes a flying leap off a desk and makes a rather shaky landing beside the blond. The whole bookshelf starts to rock madly, and both administrators just stand there staring at it, presumably trying to stop it from falling with the power of their laser-like gazes.

"Maybe they're hoping it will fall and that will solve their problem," Norton says in a totally calm and seemingly serious tone. I turn to look at him. He's shaking his head now. "I'm going to have to go in and rescue them. The kids I mean."

"You want me to help?" I offer, even though I'm not so sure my help would be appreciated by anyone in the room.

"That's okay. I can manage." He flashes a quick grin in my general direction and heads into the fray. I keep watching even though I should be going down to pick up my next group of kids. He walks into the room and straight past the dueling statues.

"Hi guys. Remember me?" he says calmly to the boys up on their teetering perch. They're starting to look like they realize this isn't quite as good an idea as they had imagined.

"No!" the blond one shouts as the shelf lurches forward. He grabs the top with both hands, knuckles white with the effort. Norton reaches out and puts his hand on the shelf, steadying it enough that neither boy falls off.

"You're that meeting dude, right? You came to my other school, right? Talked to my retarded principal, right? Talked to my mother and me, right?"

"Right. All four times."

"You're a big liar, you know? You said this place would be better. It isn't. It sucks."

"Totally sucks." The other one joins in.

"Donny, right? And...Cory?"

"How do you know our names?"

"He was at our meetings, asshole! Didn't you listen to me? Weren't you there? Are you retarded or what?"

"You're an asshole. Shut up, asshole!" Cory, or Donny, tries to take a swing, which makes the shelf move. Norton has to brace himself with both hands to keep it from falling. Mrs. Callahan and Ms. Kruger seem frozen in place.

"Whoa, guys. Why don't you come down, and we'll figure this out. I don't want a bookshelf on my head, and I don't want either of you to break your butts."

"Break our butts. Ha!" Donny, or Cory, laughs and stops swinging.

"I don't want to break my butt. Besides, this is getting boring. Let's go." They both climb down in about a second and a half.

I'm still fascinated by the show and want to stay and watch to the end, but I'm late so I head off down the hall, wondering what's going to happen next.

Cory and Donny have been at our school now for a couple of weeks. Both kids were kicked out of their former schools, and for some reason the board decided that the best thing to do with two violent, out-of-control kids desperately in need of help is to put them together full-time with a teacher who doesn't want to work with them.

Oh, and to put them in a half classroom because the school they chose for the non-self-contained class is pretty much full. To put them in the other half of *my* classroom, which is already about half the size of a regular classroom, because I am a Resource teacher, which means I am resourceful enough to teach any number of children in any size space. There's a divider (the kind that's meant to create cubicles in office spaces) down the middle of the room. The classroom has two doors so Peter's non-class can come and go without moving through my side of the room.

For the last two weeks, I have heard constant yelling and screaming and cursing.

And that's just from the teacher.

I know the boys' names because I've heard them a gazillion times, but I've never been sure which one belongs to whom. Still don't know.

"Donny! Sit down. Cory, stop hitting Donny. Donny, don't throw that. Cory, put that down. Donny, do your work. Cory, do your work. Watch your language. We don't use those words at school. Donny, leave Cory alone. Cory, leave Donny alone. Both of you, leave me alone!"

And now he's leaving them alone. What will happen to them? Will they be sent back to their other schools? Or home?

Or just to nowhere, because no one wants them?

CHAPTER 2

Time to run

I decide in the interests of my own job that I'll teach my next group in the library. Maybe I'll get lucky and there won't be any other classes in there, and I can call it a "research" period—which means my students can wander around looking like they're working, and I can think while looking like I'm teaching.

The patron saint of special ed. teachers is watching over me today, and the library is actually free. The grade eight kids start searching the shelves for fascinating books to read, their voices raised to a level that makes my head want to explode.

"Library voices!" I add to the noise by shouting. Within seconds there is relative silence.

I sit and wonder about the two athletic little guys who seem so terribly angry with life. Where did they come from?

How did they get so angry so fast? It takes most of us at least until the teen years to get truly pissed off with the world. These boys don't look any more than ten or so. How awful must their first decade of life have been to result in this much havoc?

"Hi."

I'm startled out of my reverie by the soft voice coming from behind me. Norton (what is his first name anyway?) is standing there. I wonder if the ability to sneak up on people is a prerequisite for the job or something they teach them in that fancy board office that cost untold millions of dollars— money that we were told came from a "different pot" than the money earmarked for actually helping children. There's probably a special room there just for teaching 007 skills. Probably right next door to the conference room with the $50,000 table that the board of directors bought so that each and every member could have enough personal space. After all, we can't have crowding at the board office.

Not that I'm bitter.

There are thirty-five students in our grade eight class, crammed into a space designed for about twenty. The board can't find enough money to hire another teacher so that some of those adolescent and often aromatic bodies could move to another room. Maybe it should find a more effective method of keeping its money than storing it in "pots." Obviously some of it is getting lost before it gets to the children.

"Oh, hi. How're the boys?" I ask Norton.

"They're mostly okay. Waiting for their parents to come pick them up, which is possibly not quite as okay."

We're speaking in those hushed tones reserved for

libraries, secrets, and cops on stakeouts. It's probably unnecessary, because the only other inhabitants of the room don't even seem to know we're here.

"Tough home lives, I assume?"

"Less than great, as far as I know. They're both still at home, which I guess can be looked at either way."

"Either way?"

"Good to have family who still want them. Not so good to have family who can't really look after them properly. Although, to be fair, I actually know very little about either of the boys."

"So, what now?"

"We send them home and hope no one beats them." He says this in a nonchalant tone that I have to admit shocks me. Maybe that was the point. I hadn't really gone down that road in my mind, at least not consciously. I don't like to think about the truly awful things that happen to some kids.

"I was actually just wondering what happens in terms of school. Though now I'm wondering what's going to happen at home too. Poor little guys."

He just shrugs his shoulders and shakes his head. I take that as my cue to speak again.

"It's stupid. Peter never wanted to work with them in the first place. He's a grade one teacher for heaven's sake. They moved him in there because he's got spec. ed., part one. No experience even with LD kids, let alone these guys. He has no idea, academically, emotionally. Nothing. They should at least have got someone in there with some real spec. ed. experience, someone who's worked with kids with different kinds of needs and who could at least figure out where to start. I mean, they're just kids after all. A little angrier than most, granted, but kids, right?"

"Right. Anyway, I have to go. It was nice talking to you." He leaves in the middle of my rant, and I swallow the rest of my thoughts, choking a bit on my embarrassment. He must think I'm a total idiot.

I spend the rest of the afternoon in a bit of a fog, a state that seems to go completely unnoticed by my students. Somewhat of a commentary on my teaching, I think. About ten minutes after dismissal, I'm sitting at my desk, wondering if I feel like doing some marking or getting over to the day-care early for a change, when over the intercom I hear a polite request for my presence in the office.

I'd rather have an air conditioner than an intercom, but no one asked me.

I head down to the office feeling like everyone is watching me and wondering if I'm in trouble. I wonder if the students know that we feel exactly the same way they do when the principal calls us down to the office.

"You wanted to see me?" Opening with redundancy. I know she wanted to see me, or I wouldn't have been publicly invited.

"Yes, come on in and sit down." Mrs. Callahan has painted a bigger-than-usual smile on her face, and it instantly raises my suspicions. We have never actually been on smiling terms. Not real ones anyway.

"Mr. Norton has been telling us that you're interested in taking over for Peter," she says, her smile growing even larger until it completely bisects her face. I stare at her, fascinated by the geometrical impossibility of her visage and astonished by the astronomical impossibility of her words.

"Pardon?" I hadn't even noticed Norton sitting there. He's so still; he just kind of blends into the chair. *More 007 training.*

"I was telling Mrs. Callahan how passionately you feel about the boys and their needs and how I felt you would be a good fit for them. Peter has decided to take an extended leave, and it would be easier to find someone willing to do your job than his." He smiles at me. I feel like I've been sucker-punched, and the wind's knocked out of me so that I can't speak. I just sit for a moment watching them smiling at their brilliant solution.

I look at Mrs. Callahan's bisected face and a sudden image of her running around the room after two angry little spider monkeys pops into my head. I smile in spite of myself.

"I'm glad we're all in agreement!" Mrs. Callahan says. I still haven't said anything except "pardon."

I wipe the smile off my face and try to get my mind in gear. They want me to take over Peter's job. Teaching those two louder-than-life boys who spend more time threatening the teacher than doing anything resembling schoolwork.

All because I shot my big mouth off in the library.

I don't want to change my job. I'm good at it. My students like me. Why would I want to change things for two wild boys who will likely hate me on sight?

My personal life is a total disaster right now, and I don't need my professional life to end up the same way. This is a very bad idea. I need to tell them that I don't want to do it.

"Okay. I'll do it," my mouth says out loud, completely ignoring my mind.

They both smile brightly.

"I'll arrange a visit to a Section 19 school so you can get some ideas from the staff there. They're the experts," Norton says, looking at Mrs. Callahan who nods cheerfully.

"Section school?" I have no idea what he's talking about. A section of what?

"The self-contained program over at the psych hospital. Students with significant behavioral or emotional issues sometimes need more intervention than a school can provide and are referred to a program outside of the regular system, which is covered by a specific section of the grant allocation system for spec. ed. It's a little more intense than what you'll be dealing with here, but it still might be helpful to see how they do things there."

The psych hospital? He thinks that I'll learn how to teach these boys by visiting a psych hospital?

"That sounds wonderful," Mrs. Callahan chirps happily.

No it doesn't. It sounds terrifying.

They both look so very pleased with themselves. I'm glad they're enjoying mapping out my life.

It seems I have just agreed to a job that I don't want to do.

Maybe that Section school can help me with my mental health issues. My mind seems to have left the building. Maybe if I run out of here fast enough, I'll be able to grab it before it's gone completely.

Maybe I'll even catch up to Peter.

CHAPTER 3

Non-violent sounds good

I wake up the next morning to find brilliant sunshine pouring in my bedroom window. I lie still, letting it wash over me, lulled by its warm rays into a general feeling of contentment. If I could, I would purr. Only a cat can truly express the ultimate feeling of basking in the heat of the sun.

The ringing of the phone interrupts my pursuit of doing nothing. Before I answer, I take the time to wonder who would be calling me at 6:30 a.m.

"Hello?" My heart is beating a little faster. Calls this early can't be good news.

"Hi! It's Mrs. Callahan. I hope I didn't wake you. I figured you'd already be up and getting those lovely daughters of yours ready for school."

"Just getting ready to do that." *Callahan is calling me at home? Now what does she want?*

"Well, you can take your time today, because you don't have to come in to school."

"Excuse me?" I heard her, but she isn't making sense. Maybe I'm still asleep and dreaming. Maybe yesterday was a dream too, and I didn't really agree to turn my life inside out.

"You don't have to come to school today." She repeats it and continues speaking. "You're going down to the psych hospital to take a look at their Section class. It was set up for you last night, but I didn't get the message until just now. You are expected any time this morning, so just get there when you can. You're going to spend a bit of time with a teacher there to get some ideas. Not that we're starting a Section class."

No, of course not. After all, according to Norton, a Section class is for students who are removed from the regular school population because of extreme emotional-slash-behavioral issues. Cory and Donny are right there in a regular school—hidden away in the other half of the Resource room.

"Okay. What happens to the boys today then? Is Peter back?"

"No. Peter's taking a bit of time off. The boys are just going to be at home today."

"You suspended them?"

"Not officially. They'll be back Monday. I will see you Monday, as well. Have a good day." And she hangs up without waiting for a response. Which is just as well, because I can't think of a polite one.

The students are unofficially suspended because they were doing the things that brought them to our school in the first place. They're staying home because no one is there to teach them.

And I'm spending my day at a school in a psych hospital because I don't have the slightest idea how to teach them.

Monday should be fun. I can't wait. Cats don't go to school. No wonder they can purr and we can't.

What am I getting myself into?

This is probably really, really bad timing. I'm going through a divorce and trying to adjust to life as a single mother. My daughters need me to be on my A-game so I can help them through this time without their being scarred for life.

I already have a job that I'm good at and that I like, one that's challenging enough not to bore me, but not so challenging that it wipes me out.

I don't think I'll be able to say the same about the non-class. I mean, I've had troubled students in my Resource periods. I've had to sit in on meetings that talk about home lives that make me want to cry in front of everyone in the room. But these boys? They redefine the concept of troubled. They're the angriest, most damaged little guys I've ever seen outside of a TV screen. What can I possibly do for them? I'm a mess. I don't even know who I am these days. I need to get myself figured out so that I can be a decent mother to my girls. Is this the right time for me to be taking on a virtually impossible task at work?

I take advantage of the extra time and keep both girls home until school time. It's nice to have a leisurely breakfast with them. Teaching is the world's best profession for a mom—decent hours, same holidays as the kids—but it's still hectic enough trying to get one to school and the other to daycare without forgetting to feed them or make sure they're both wearing shoes.

✗

I arrive at the hospital at around nine. It's a throwback, a large, ugly building that looks like something left there by mistake. Gray, regimented walls hold rows of haughty windows staring disapprovingly at the frilly gardens and pretty fences decorating the more frivolous homes lining the rest of street. A thin edging of precisely cut grass stretches across the front of the building, bisected by a pathway of pavement that matches the walls. Large, forbidding double doors stand at attention, making sure that no unwelcome visitors find their way in—and that no one who belongs there manages to find their way out.

It's hard to imagine a school in there. Even harder to imagine children actually living inside.

Maybe the inside is nicer than the out. Can't be worse.

I walk up to doors so big that they make me feel a bit like Alice down the rabbit hole, shrinking into nothingness. What am I doing here? I'm awkward and out of place. Nervous.

Stop it. Grow up! This is a hospital. Inside there is a school. Filled with children. I'm a teacher. I can handle this.

I grab the handle and pull. Nothing happens. Of course not. It's locked. Keeping me out or them in?

There's a buzzer with an intercom over at the side. I press it and identify myself to the disembodied voice that welcomes me. I'm told to wait until someone comes to escort me to the school area of the building.

This is not making me less nervous.

Several more minutes pass before the door finally opens and a rather stern-looking man gestures for me to come in.

"I'm John Hansen, Principal. I'll give you a bit of background and then take you down to meet the class. I understand you'll be teaching a behavior class at your school."

"Well, they aren't exactly calling it that, but it's close enough, I guess."

"Do you have any background in behavioral strategies? Non-violent crisis intervention?"

Non-violent sounds good.

"Um, no. This is all rather sudden. And not really all that well planned. That's why I'm here, I suppose." I try a self-effacing smile, but it doesn't seem to impress him any more than my words do. He just looks at me like I'm nuts—which is about right.

"Well, perhaps we can speak to your principal about at least getting you the weekend course. In the meantime, we can try to give you a few helpful ideas."

Weekend course does not sound good. On weekends, I'm a mom. I don't say it out loud though. He's already unimpressed with me.

"We have six classes here at the moment," he says, unlocking the next series of doors before leading me down a quiet hallway. There's still no feeling at all that we're anywhere near a school—or a child. So far, the building is as gray inside as it is on the outside. Sterile and quiet.

"All of our students currently live in the cottages. We have no non-residents at this time. We're at full capacity with a rather extensive waiting list. All of the students are under psychiatric care, and we work closely with medical and social services staff on programming."

"That sounds...good." *That sounds good? A school full of*

pint-sized psych patients sounds good? I think I'll just tape my mouth shut until I go home again.

"It's the only way to help the children. They need full care. It's not just about learning how to read and write. They have to learn how to live." His words are colored with compassion, and for a second I see the teacher underneath the administrator.

"Here we are." We're at another set of locked doors. I guess they don't have too many runaways. He unlocks the doors and opens them. The noise hits me in a wave, and it's obvious that we're finally at the school. Voices come flying out at us—yelling, laughing, talking, crying, and some screaming, all blending into the symphony of childhood. The sound makes me smile, and my nerves settle at last.

"We have the six classrooms, a small library, and a life-skills room. No gym, unfortunately, but occasionally we have use of the facilities at the local recreation center," he says, as I follow him down the hall. "Here is Ms. Desmond's room. Ms. Desmond!" He raises his voice at the door of a classroom filled with activity. I can see about ten students in the room, most of them sitting at desks doing some kind of work. One child is being held by a staff member who has his arms wrapped around her from the back. The girl is screaming a rather awesome stream of profanity at him while he calmly talks to her.

"Non-violent crisis intervention." Mr. Hansen gestures toward the scene as if his words explain everything. They don't. I see a weekend of learning instead of mothering in my future.

"Hi and welcome." A young woman is at the door, smiling

at me while keeping both eyes on her class at the same time.

"You've caught us at a relatively quiet moment. Only Jeanie is having a bit of trouble." She gestures at the little girl still screaming her inventive list of swear words.

"Who is that with her? An educational assistant?"

"No, I don't have an EA in this class. Actually she's a trained child and youth worker. Couldn't do my job without them. Do you have someone who will be working with you?"

"We haven't got that far. Only two students, and no one is admitting it's a class yet. So I don't have any idea what comes next."

"That sounds like fun. Anyway, I wasn't sure what you needed from me, so I figured I'd just try to show you a typical day, and we could talk at lunch."

"That'd be fine."

I spend the rest of the morning trying to fade into the background, yet watching in complete fascination. It's a class full of Cory- and Donny-styled children, all of them continuously edging toward their boiling points, ready to blow the top off of any given situation.

The teacher stays completely calm in the middle of all of this intense emotion. The heat emanating from the children seems to roll up around her and down off her back without leaving any burn marks at all. Either she's a master teacher or a wonderful actress. Regardless, her calm in the midst of their storm seems to keep the morning moving forward.

"Any questions?" she asks me when lunchtime comes and she has a few moments away from the kids.

"Only about a million!" I laugh and she smiles.

"I know how you feel. I couldn't believe this place the

first day I saw it. I had no thought of anything remotely like this when I started teaching."

"Me either. But it's…fascinating, I guess. The kids are so…raw."

"That's a perfect word! I'll have to remember that one. They are exactly that. Raw. Unprepared for life. No false pretenses. No hypocrisy. Everything just comes out the way they think it. Unfiltered. And socially unacceptable."

"Which is how they end up here. Do they all come from terrible homes? Is that how they become like this?"

"Not necessarily although many of them do have rough backgrounds one way or another. But the reasons they end up so hurt and angry and uncontrolled are so much more complicated than just a difficult home life. Honestly, I wouldn't know where to start to try to explain what little I know about it."

"What kind of special training do you have to do this?"

"Not much. Spec. ed., part one. A couple of weekend courses. Non-violent crisis intervention. Behavior management. That kind of thing."

"Was it enough?" I can't imagine a couple of weekend courses being enough to cope with all of this.

"No. I had no idea what to do at first. Most days I come in here still wondering what I'm going to do to get through the day. But I keep on reminding myself that they're just kids."

"The teachers in my school see them as crazy kids who bring too many problems with them," I tell her. "They want them to disappear into a place like this."

"Some kids *do* need to be here, in my opinion. They need

a safe place, away from everything and everyone, where they can figure out how to survive out there. So many of them just don't have the tools to do that. I don't know if this will be helpful or not, but there's a simple story from a workshop I went to that really stuck with me. Do you have kids?"

"Yes. Two girls."

"Well, think back to when they were just learning to talk, just trying to figure out how to use language to communicate. Your baby's thirsty and asks you for juice. She might say something like 'ju ju' and point to the kitchen. What's your response?"

"I would get super excited and run for the juice jug, saying, 'Yes, juice' in a really loud, clear voice. And I would declare that my kid was a genius." She looks at me and laughs.

"Exactly. But imagine if, instead, you just ignored her. She keeps saying 'ju ju,' and you keep ignoring her, and she gets louder and louder. Finally, in frustration, she starts to scream and cry. You get her a cup of juice to shut her up. And what does she learn?"

"Screaming and crying gets results."

"Yeah. It's a really simple example and only tells one of the endless stories that these kids come with. But it's a starting point to understanding some of them, the ones who literally don't know how to behave any other way. The wrong behavior was reinforced so many times when they were young, for whatever reason—abuse, neglect, ignorance—that they don't know anything else. Of course there are other factors, like mental health issues that seem to have nothing to do with environment at all—kids from nice homes with loving parents who still can't get through a day without living through a crisis or two. The list is actually pretty endless, and I'm no expert. I do have some books you could try."

"That would be extremely helpful! And I need all the help I can get."

We talk some more, and I watch her teach some more and leave feeling even less prepared than before I came. I can't imagine coming anywhere close to her level of expertise.

Then again, I only have two students.

What could possibly go wrong?

CHAPTER 4

G-R-E-A-T *spells great!*

Suddenly it's Monday. My Resource kids have already been told that they will have a supply teacher until a permanent replacement can be found—even though I had wanted to tell them myself. And I find myself on the other side of the divider in my own classroom, trying not to be nervous as I attempt to set up the classroom to look like…well, a classroom.

Peter had this theory, apparently supported by someone he consulted from the dinosaur age, that the room should be completely barren. Nothing on the walls that the students could rip off. No attractive books that pages could be torn out of. Nothing interesting to play with that could be broken or used as a weapon.

In Peter's defense, after listening to everything that went on in here the first few weeks of the school year, I can only imagine the rampant destruction that would have ensued had he given them something to destroy.

On the other hand, after listening to everything that went on in here the last few weeks, I am imagining the great pride the students will feel when presented with a classroom that looks welcoming and interesting. I see it as my way of telling the boys that things are different now, that I trust them to respect their world and, by extension, me.

And while I'm at it, maybe I'll see if I can sell them some life insurance.

So here I am, doing what I can to decorate my half of a classroom with whatever bits and pieces I can find. I didn't want to take anything of mine from my other "classroom," because I didn't want my Resource students to have to face too much change all at once.

A couple of lame posters and a few even lamer books later, and my half room is ready.

Now I have to get myself ready.

I've already looked at the work that the kids were doing. Mostly grade one worksheets, from what I can tell. Both boys are ten, with Donny turning eleven in about a week. There's no clear record of actual learning potential in their student record files and very little information about their personal lives. So basically I'm doing a swan dive off the top of a cliff without any idea how deep the water is below.

Peter also had them on some sort of token reward system whereby they earned points for tickets that would turn into toys if they got enough of them. According to the chart on the wall—the only decoration in the room when I walked in this morning—no one has ever earned a toy.

I took the chart down and got rid of the tickets and the cheap plastic toys. I think I'll do things a different way. I haven't figured out exactly what that's going to be yet. I'm hoping it will come to me.

But they're kids, right? Just kids. I can't be nervous about working with a couple of kids. This is what I do...who I am. I'm a teacher. I'm a mom. Everything I do is about kids. Has been since I was one myself. I must have some skills by now.

"So, all set?" Mrs. Callahan is standing at the door with a big smile on her face. I can't summon up the energy to pretend to smile back.

"Not really. This is all pretty sudden. I have to get my head around it. At least it's only two kids though."

"Oh, about that. We have a meeting after school with the parent of a new student. From what I gather, he'll fit in just fine here. We'll give you a few days to settle the two boys who are already here and then get him going."

"Here? With me? In this half of a non-class?"

"Yes. We can't really get proper funding with a two-to-one ratio. We need to fill you up a bit." She's already moving away by the time the last word pops out of her mouth. She does that—drops a bomb and then gets out of the way just as it detonates.

Three kids. What is it the teacher said to me Friday? Multiply the number you have by at least three, and you have the true amount of attention these kids need. So three kids equals nine. Nine to one. The odds are getting worse by the second.

I don't have an EA or a youth worker. I don't even have a time-out room.

I used to have a time-out chair for my youngest when she was little. It was a place she was supposed to sit and think, which was code for "you're being punished by sitting on this chair when you'd rather be playing." At the psych hospital school, they have a whole room for kids to sit and think in. Except there, the kids don't sit alone. The time-out room is actually a place for the students who need it to de-escalate with the help of a staff member who holds them until they can hold themselves, someone who talks them down from whatever heights their anger and pain have driven them to. Ms. Desmond had told me that I would have to persuade admin to find a way for me to have a time-out room, because my kids would need a place to de-escalate.

I look around my space. Three kids and me in here. There's a closet at the back with craft supplies in it, but I think it would be a tight squeeze for me and a student in there. Not much de-escalation going on when you can't breathe.

So, in ten minutes I have two behaviorally challenged, most likely emotionally disturbed, boys arriving to be educated in a half-assed room with no program, no real psych support, and no time-out room.

There's only me.

And I don't know what I'm doing.

"The cabs are here." The intercom interrupts my panic attack. The boys in my non-class can't be on a regular bus, so they're sent in cabs with unsuspecting drivers. Sounds safe to me.

I walk down the hall, doing my best to affect a confident stride. Can't let them see I'm scared. I try, unsuccessfully, to plaster a smiling expression on my face, which ends up making me feel like how a gargoyle looks. Probably scare the poor little buggers right back into the cabs.

"Who the fuck are you?" Donny looks at me with an expression that makes it pretty clear he isn't afraid of me. Or anyone else, for that matter.

"I'm Ms. S. Your new teacher." I decide to ignore the f-word. Not going to start my first day with a fight. I used only the first letter of my name because I've been listening. The boys have always called Peter "Mr. D," and I think I've heard them call Callahan "Mrs. C." I thought I'd gain points by speaking their language.

"Where the fuck is Mr. D?" Cory spits on the ground just in front of my shoe. Pretty sure he missed his target.

"He has been offered an opportunity to teach elsewhere," I answer in this strange, formal voice that I usually reserve for job interviews. Which, come to think of it, is probably pretty appropriate here, because I'm fairly certain these two will be the ones to decide if I keep this particular job.

"He's been offered a job elsewhere. Which means he's a chicken shit and just didn't want to teach us anymore." Donny shakes his head with as much disgust as anyone could possibly put into a headshake.

"Yeah, chicken shit." Cory shakes his head too. Starting to see a pattern here. If this was a cop show and these two were suspects, I'd be aiming my questions at Cory. Easier to break.

"Well, he's not here, and I am, so let's get down to the classroom and see how we get along."

See how we get along? What is wrong with me! Now I sound like I'm on a date. A really, really bad date.

I start to walk, breathing a sigh of relief when they actually come with me.

"What's all this stuff?" Donny strolls around the room, looking at the posters on the walls and the few books on the shelves that aren't math or science texts.

"This is your room. I wanted it to look…more pleasant, I guess."

"Mr. D didn't like stuff on the walls. Said we would just rip it off, so why bother."

"He said that?" The words come out of my mouth without remembering the vow I made at about three o'clock this morning to not talk to the boys about anything Peter did or didn't do. I don't want comparisons. I want a clean start.

"Yup. He said we couldn't control our impulses, and so it wasn't worth making things nice or whatever."

"Well, I don't see things exactly that way. I think you can control your impulses enough to leave a few posters on the wall."

The two boys look at each other. I'm no mind reader, but I don't have to be to see that they're trying to decide whether or not to run around the room, ripping and tearing and proving me wrong. After what seems like forever, Donny nods almost imperceptibly. Cory nods back, completely perceptibly. I have to get that kid in a poker game some time.

"I have a poster at home. Can I bring it?" Donny's arms are crossed, and he's glaring at me, ready for the no.

"Of course! That would make the room yours. Great!" *Now I'm a cheerleader. G-R-E-A-T spells great!*

Donny smiles and nods slowly, and I realize that I probably just got played. I didn't ask what poster he had at home.

I didn't talk about appropriate pictures for school. I've been brush-stroked into a corner by a pro.

Ms. Desmond warned me to watch for this. She said that contrary to popular belief, most of the students she worked with were really bright and could manipulate adults better than other adults could. That their lack of performance in school had nothing to do with a lack of intelligence.

I'm the one lacking intelligence. Ten minutes into day one and I'm pretty sure I've just agreed to decorate my class with either pornography or profanity.

"Okay. I want to talk with you a bit about how I'd like to see things operate around here, and then we'll get to some work. Okay?" *Shit! I broke another vow already.* Two more, actually. Number one: never, ever use language you don't want them to use, even inside your head; and number two: never, ever, ever say "Okay?" as if you are giving them a choice, when you aren't.

"Not really. I don't like work. Stupid pile of crap."

"Totally stupid pile of crap."

"Well, that's one of the things I want to talk to you about. I'm starting your programs over. We're going to try some different types of work than you're used to. I don't really know where either of you are at, so we're going to have to experiment a bit with different things. So say good-bye to the old work." I pick up the pile of worksheets that are mostly scribbled over with big, black slash marks and throw them ceremoniously in the recycling bin.

"Hey, wait a minute. I want to do that!" Donny runs over and grabs the pile as it falls into the bin. He gestures to Cory to come over and hands him some papers. For the next few minutes, the only sound in the room is the ripping and crumpling of two weeks' of worthless worksheets.

This isn't exactly what I had planned for first period, but they seem pretty happy, so I decide that maybe it's all right to let it go.

Once the worksheets are thoroughly destroyed, we try some hands-on math activities that turn into games—gladiator-style games that involve throwing things around the room and shoving each other to the ground. I manage to get them both back up on their feet without any blood being spilled, and we move on to language.

Neither boy seems to be willing—or perhaps able—to read, so I spend most of the next forty minutes reading to them while they fidget on the floor, poking at each other and rolling their eyes at me when they think I'm focused on the book. I wonder again at the scarcity of academic information in their files. Has anyone wondered about whether or not learning issues are getting in the way? Even kids without serious emotional problems can go down the "bad" behavior road if they can't do the work. Feeling stupid doesn't exactly make a kid want to be well-behaved.

Noon rolls around, and I realize that there isn't anything in place for proper lunch supervision. I can't take them to the lunchroom with the other kids. I can't send them out on the schoolyard either. It didn't even occur to me to ask what happens at break times.

I don't really have much planned for the afternoon. I thought I would see how the morning went and then figure out the rest of the day on my lunch break.

There's no choice. At least not today. It's me. All me, all

the time. I'm not going to have one single second of a break. I can't even go to the bathroom.

This is crazy. I need to talk to Mrs. Callahan about this after school.

Oh, right. I'm talking to Mrs. Callahan today after school about adding another student to my non-class. I'm sure she'll figure out a way to disappear before I get a chance to mention anything else—like peeing or eating.

Now I have to figure it out while trying to keep them busy for an hour in a mostly empty classroom. I'm afraid to take them outside in case one or both of them run away or beat someone up. I can't take them to the gym because I didn't think to book it. I don't have any games or toys in the room.

I'm going to have to resort to the teacher cheat of watching a video for now. Assuming I can use the intercom to find someone who can go and see if there's a TV available. And assuming that the boys will actually slow down long enough to watch a video.

And I'd better do it fast, because they've already stopped eating and are starting to throw their leftovers in each other's faces.

"Donny! Sit down. Cory, stop hitting Donny. Donny, don't throw that. Cory, put that down. Donny, leave Cory alone. Cory, leave Donny alone."

Both of you, leave me alone. At least long enough so that I can figure out what to do.

If I start running now, there still might be a chance of catching up to Peter.

CHAPTER 5

What do you say to a whale?

"Dickhead." The woman sitting across from me in Callahan's office smiles pleasantly.

"Excuse me?"

"His one word. The one that he uses. It's *dickhead*." She puts a slight emphasis on the word this time just in case I still don't understand.

"The only word that he uses at school is dickhead?" I'm not sure why I repeat it. Twice is enough in one conversation, I think. I look over at Mrs. Callahan, who is smiling benevolently at no one in particular.

"Yes. I'm not sure why," the parent of my soon-to-be new student continues. "I don't know where he heard it. Certainly not from me!" She shakes her head for emphasis. I nod to let her know that I firmly believe that her son could never, ever have heard such a word from her. It's a well-known fact that parents are incapable of using profane language of any kind. Children *always* learn it from someone else.

"Well, we'll just take it one step at a time. There are lots of good consonant sounds and even a couple of vowels in dickhead that can certainly start us off."

She nods at me as if I have said something wise instead of completely ridiculous. "Well, I'm sure he's in the right place. Oh, and one other thing. He doesn't like sleeves."

"Sleeves?"

"Yes, you know, like on shirts and sweaters and things. Sleeves." She pulls on her own fuchsia blouse just in case I still don't get it. I nod, patting the sleeve of my own black sweater before I can stop myself.

"So don't ever loan him a shirt with sleeves. He becomes very upset. At home, I just cut the sleeves off. He likes it that way."

I nod again. I've been nodding so much that my neck is sore, but I'm at a loss. I want to ask her why she doesn't just buy sleeveless shirts, but I'm a little afraid of the answer.

"I knew you'd understand. He has a few little…quirks. Without a formal diagnosis, it's been really difficult to figure out what to do for him. It's just that no one seems to be able to figure him out, you know? But I feel really good about this placement. He'll do really well here. Most schools don't have these classes anymore, you know."

"Well, Ms. McNally, it was explained to you that this is an integration-based program. We aren't technically a class. Kevin will be spending time in a class with same-aged peers when he's ready."

That's the theory anyway. For all of them. Hard to imagine at the moment.

"Oh yes. I know. But at least he'll have somewhere safe to start out and somewhere to go if it doesn't work out in the regular classroom. I think you and he will get along just fine."

"Yes, it's too bad he couldn't have come with you today so I could meet him and show him the room before he starts next week."

"Next week? Oh no. I thought he was going to start tomorrow!" She looks from me to Mrs. Callahan and back again. I look from her to Mrs. Callahan and back again. Mrs. Callahan smiles benevolently at no one in particular.

"Oh yes," she says, turning to me. "I forgot to let you know. We did decide that Kevin should start tomorrow rather than later on. You've had a great first day with the boys who are here already. I'm sure it'll be fine." She still isn't looking directly at me. I wish she would. The phrase "if looks could kill" springs to mind.

A good first day—if you don't count the profanity, the wrestling match during math, the food fight at lunch, and an afternoon mostly spent watching a video with no educational value before almost missing the cabs at the end of the day because neither of them would come when I told them to. But no bones were broken nor blood spilled, so I guess some people might see that as a good day. It's all relative.

Ms. Desmond told me that there might be a honeymoon period at the beginning. If this is the honeymoon, I don't think I want to see the marriage.

"Tomorrow's perfect. He's burned a few bridges at his current school, so he's just sitting at home right now. Not that he actually lit any fires. Or at least not many. Anyway, I won't keep you any longer. If you have any questions, you know how to reach me."

Kevin's mother picks up her purse and scurries out of the room before I can open my mouth. I have a lot more questions! I look over at Mrs. Callahan, but she's already up and moving out the door.

"Thanks. See you tomorrow!" she chirps cheerfully.

If Donny were here, he'd call her a chicken shit.

✗

Tuesday arrives after a sleepless night filled with dire predictions about the inevitable combustive outcome of adding a new student who is going to start the second day of my new professional life by calling Donny and Cory dickheads.

Kevin arrives first, dropped off by his mom because there hasn't been enough time to arrange a cab. He's a short, round little guy with a mop of hair that hangs down far enough that I wonder if he can see. I can't tell if he's even trying to look at me, but I hold my hand out anyway.

"Good morning, Kevin. Welcome to your new school."

"Dickhead," he mutters, keeping both of his hands firmly in his pockets. My hand is still sticking out, looking conspicuously awkward. I try to bring it back in gracefully, folding both hands together in front of me like a well-mannered school girl. His mother laughs a little and ruffles his already ruffled hair.

"Bye, sweetie. Have a good day," she sings to him, giving him a kiss on the cheek, which he immediately wipes off with the back of his hand, which he then wipes on the front of his jeans. She looks at me with a smile that's almost bright enough to camouflage the quick flash of sadness in her eyes.

"Good luck," she says softly and heads out the front door. I watch her for a second and then look back at Kevin. He's looking down at the floor. Or his shoes. Or maybe he's just looking at his hair, which is hanging directly in front of his eyes.

"Okay, well, I guess we'll head down to get the other guys. Their cabs will be here any second." He doesn't seem too impressed. He's still just standing there, hands in pockets, head bent toward the ground.

"So, follow me!" I start down the hall, not sure what I'll do if he decides to stay where he is.

I walk slowly for about thirty seconds before looking back. He's still there. Great. The boys are going to be here any second, and there's no one else to pick them up.

"Kevin? We're going this way." I try gentle authority instead of obnoxious enthusiasm. He stands still for a few seconds more and then slowly starts down toward me. I'm not sure how he's figuring out which way to go. Echolocation maybe? We make our way slowly down to the door leading out to the cabs, where he stops short. I head out to get the other two boys, hoping that he stays where he is.

The other two have already arrived and are just getting ready to make alternate plans for the day when I reach them.

"Sorry, I didn't mean to be late on our second day! I have someone for you to meet!" *The cheerleader's back. Buffy the Kid-Slayer.* They both look at me with suspicious eyes. Donny looks past me to where Kevin is standing.

"It's okay. It's just a kid," he says. I'm not sure if he's

telling Cory or himself. The three of us go into the building and stand in front of Kevin.

"Kevin, this is Cory and this is Donny. They will be working with you."

"Hey man," says Donny.

"Dickhead." Kevin says it fast and without particular inflection. He doesn't look up. I look at the boys, bracing myself.

"Cool," says Donny.

"Cool," says Cory, with just the hint of a giggle.

I was expecting fireworks—or at least a punch in the face. But obviously I totally underestimated them. Maybe, on some level, they understand that there's no real malice in his word choice.

Or maybe they actually think he's cool. Or that dickheads are cool.

Best just to accept it and not over-analyze.

✗

During the next few days, their instant acceptance of Kevin turns into an interesting kind of protective instinct. It also gives Cory and Donny someone else to pay attention to, and they actually get through an hour or two each day without throwing anything at each other or threatening to beat each other's brains in. From what I've seen and heard so far, Cory and Donny are generally examples of Darwinism at its purest; survival of the fittest, adapting to anything and everything with fierce self-protection. I doubt that protecting anyone else has ever been a part of the plan. But somehow Kevin's presence in the room has started to change the dynamic.

Looking out for number one has shifted a little bit to looking out for Kevin.

"Kevin, I expect you to at least try to do this work. I know you can do some of it because I have your work folder from your other school." I put the simple worksheet in front of him and hand him a nice fat red pencil. Kevin actually has a pretty complete student file. I know he has multiple learning issues that have only started to be properly examined within the school system. Kevin's behavior is mostly passive-resistant in nature, which makes him pretty hard to test, but some of the staff who have worked with him in the past have managed to get him to comply a bit, and I have a decent idea as to a starting point. The problem here is that Kevin has different ideas, none of which involve doing anything that I ask him to do.

"Ms. S, you need to back off him. He doesn't like seat work." Cory looks at me as if I'm stupid for not figuring that out myself.

"I don't think you particularly like seat work either, but you still do it. Sometimes."

"I know, but he's different. It's like, harder for him and stuff." I'm torn between being pleased to see Cory standing up for someone other than himself and the need to exert some kind of authority over Kevin.

"How do you know that?" I ask, pushing the envelope just a little, a calculated risk that is most likely going to backfire in loudly spectacular ways.

"Baby told me."

Now what? "Baby? Who's Baby?"

"I'm Baby!" A high-pitched, vaguely familiar voice comes

from the general vicinity of Kevin's desk. Cory and Donny start to giggle, but quietly, so that they don't miss anything. I look at Kevin, but he's still staring down at the paper on his desk without moving.

This is one of those defining moments in a teacher's life—the moment when I can take control of the situation and make wise and informed choices that will show my students that I am in control.

"Okay, Baby, show yourself. I would like to talk to you."

The giggling intensifies.

"I'm afraid of you. I have to stay away."

"You don't need to be afraid of me. I just want to talk to you." I lean down beside Kevin's desk. I have no idea what to do here. I'm way out of my depth and sinking fast.

"Dickhead!" he says, more loudly than usual but in the same deep, guttural voice that he has been using every day.

"He's not Baby!" Cory's voice lets me know that now he's sure I'm stupid. The giggling has become full-fledged laughter.

"It's okay, Kev. You can show her. I don't think she'll do anything too stupid." Donny says this in a gentle voice that I haven't heard before. Kevin looks over at him, and Donny nods. I'm mesmerized by the moment. I need to grab it and freeze it so I can remember it the next time he decides to tell me into which of my orifices I should shove his undone work.

Kevin reaches into his desk and pulls out what looks like a stuffed killer whale.

"I'm Baby," says the whale in her high-pitched voice. At least, I think it's a her.

The laughter dies an immediate death as the boys suck in

their breath, watching me to see what I'm going to do.

Maybe everyone else met Baby at lunchtime, when Mrs. Jackson was covering for me. She's the new Resource teacher who replaced me. She's been roped into watching my boys at lunchtime every day so that I can leave the room long enough to grab some food. I'm supposed to stay away a full forty minutes, but I don't think it's fair to leave her alone with them that long. She didn't sign up for this. I'm the only one who's that crazy.

And now I'm face to face with a talking stuffed whale.

I have no idea what Norton would tell me to do here. He is supposed to be my consultant. Maybe I should call him for a consult with regard to a stuffed killer whale called Baby who talks a whole lot better than a strange little boy called Kevin. But the kids are still holding their breath, so I don't really have time.

"Hello, Baby. I'm glad to meet you," I say, holding out my hand without thinking about why. Kevin gives me a look that makes me think maybe he has some laughter tucked away inside somewhere. He hands me the whale and everyone breathes.

"Hi," says Baby.

"So, you're Kevin's friend," I say, trying to keep the conversation going. *What does one say to a whale anyway?*

"I'm Baby."

"Yes, I know."

"Not Kevin's friend. Just Baby. Just me."

"Okay, Baby. I'm glad to meet you." *I already said that.* I'm pretty sure I can hear Donny laughing into his hand. Apparently I really don't know what to say to a whale.

"Kevin doesn't like this kind of pencil. It's too long, and he can't hold it. He needs the rubber thing." The whale is looking at me as if I'm stupid for not understanding what her role is here.

"The rubber thing?" I'm still talking directly to the whale, who is still staring at me with beady little eyes that judge my every word.

"The rubber thing that goes on the pencil." If she had a head, she would shake it at me. But she's really just a body with a mouth that doesn't move when she talks.

Not that she's the one talking. I know that. Really.

"Pencil grip," Donny says, swallowing his laughter as he gets up and goes to the side cupboard. "I think it's over here somewhere." He rummages around for a bit and comes out holding a rubber pencil grip designed to help kids with motor difficulties hold their pencils more comfortably. He brings it over to me, and I put it on Kevin's pencil.

"Thanks," says Baby as she disappears back into Kevin's desk.

"You're welcome," I say to the top of Kevin's desk. "Okay, everyone, back to work. Kevin, I'll help you get started on this worksheet."

"Dickhead," says Kevin.

CHAPTER 6

Family matters

"Get the fuck out of my face!" Donny turns his head away, looking at the wall.

"I'm not in your face. I'm in front of it. Stupid." Cory slithers over to the wall so he's still directly in Donny's line of vision.

They both came in completely wired today—even more than usual. I was a couple of seconds late picking them up because Mrs. Callahan decided to pull me over for another one of her chats, and by the time I got there, something had happened between the boys that neither of them will talk to me about. The only witness was Kevin, but I knew if I asked him, all I would get is "dickhead." I thought about asking the whale but decided I wasn't that desperate yet.

I might be now.

"Cory, leave Donny alone and go sit down." I'm using a calm but authoritative voice...I think. I can't really hear myself because I'm breathing too loudly. I'm pretty sure they're about to have a fight. I hate it when they do that. I don't like to get physical with the kids, but sometimes there isn't a choice. I've asked Mrs. Callahan about the whole child-worker thing, and she keeps telling me she'll call Mr. Norton and get back to me.

I'm going to have to call him myself. Now might be a good time.

"I'm not doing anything to him. I'm just sitting here." Cory is on the floor beside Donny's desk.

"I'm done with this crap. Seriously." Donny jumps to his feet, and his desk flies across the room. Paper scatters everywhere as the desk crashes loudly to the floor.

"Think you're scary or something? Fucking loser, man." Cory is on his feet. He grabs the edge of his desk and starts to lift it. I grab the other side and shove it back down.

"You are *not* throwing this desk."

"Oh yeah. Right! Fag-face can throw his and that's all cool with you. Right? He can do whatever he wants."

He's still trying to lift the desk, and it's taking all my strength to keep it down on the floor. I'm on the opposite side of the room from the intercom, so I can't call for reinforcements. I can't hear anything on the other side of the divider, so my replacement must have her kids in the library or something. I can't yell for help because that would make me sound like I need help. I can't let them know that I'm not in control.

I am not in control. Of anything.

I decide to sit on the desk, hoping my superior weight will be enough to stop Cory's efforts. With my hands free, I feel a bit less trapped by the situation.

"I hate this stupid place. I hate both of you. You're all assholes!" Donny is screaming by now. Someone must be hearing this. Someone has to come.

"Donny. Just try to calm down. We can talk about this." My voice is shaking, and I pray they don't hear the tremors.

"Calm down? You want me to fucking calm down? Fine!"

Before I can even register what he's doing, he springs forward and punches Cory in the side of the head. Hard. I leap from the desk to intervene, but he's already out the door and running down the hall. I take a second to make sure Cory is still conscious. He's looking a bit stunned and slides down onto the floor, holding his head tightly as if he's afraid Donny knocked it loose.

I step over him and press the intercom. The office admin's calm and professional voice asks if she can help me. Once I explain the situation, she assures me she'll let Mrs. Callahan know.

Oh, good. Now I feel safe.

Cory is crying. The angry, aggressive pain-in-Donny's-butt is gone. All that's left is a hurt little boy sobbing on my floor.

"Hey, it's okay. You'll be okay." Empty words.

"No it's not. Nothing is. Nothing ever is." And he cries and cries, water pouring out of him with the force of an opened fire hydrant on a hot summer's day in the city. He's hugging himself and rocking back and forth. I watch him for a second, and all of the school system's rules against physically comforting children go spinning through my mind.

"I'm sorry you got hurt." It's the only thing I can think to say as I wrap my arms around him and rock him back and forth like I do with my daughters when they're hurt or afraid. He lets me do it for about five seconds until he remembers that he's super tough, and then he pushes me away.

"Donny is an asshole," he says, getting to his feet.

"Dickhead," says Kevin. We both look at him. I had forgotten he was here. He doesn't even look over at us.

"That's right, Kev. Donny is a dickhead and an asshole. At least you're cool."

"Dickhead."

And just like that, it's calm. Cory goes over to sit beside Kevin, and look at a comic book that Kevin has hidden in his desk. I can't leave to check on Donny, so I clean up his mess instead.

I wish I had some kind of crystal ball so I could see what happens in their lives before and after school each day. All I know about Donny is that he lives with his mom and that there have been some concerns about the quality of her parenting and suggestions that she could be at the root of Donny's behavior issues. But I don't know any real details. I do know that Donny doesn't have any concerns. He talks about his mother as if she's his favorite person in the world, the queen of his personal castle.

Maybe Cory said something to Donny about his mother this morning. Criticizing each other's mothers is a favorite form of verbal torture. That would certainly have caused a fight.

About forty-five minutes later, Norton comes to the door. Neither of the boys pays him any attention. They're finished with the comic and are pretending to read a couple of books I handed to them. Cory has a nice big lump on the side of his head but otherwise seems all right physically.

"I just wanted to update you on Donny." He's using a library voice so the boys won't overhear, but they're not interested.

"Thanks. No one else has bothered to." My voice sounds petulant, but I don't care. I'm tired and mad.

"Yeah, well. That's something else that needs to be dealt with. Anyway, first things first. Donny has been officially suspended for three days. After he left here, he basically trashed everything he could until I got here and restrained him. Lucky I was close by. Anyway, he's finally calmed down, so I'm taking him home now."

"And then what?"

"And then he comes back when it's over, I guess."

"No, I meant is he safe at home? I know there are concerns about his mom. Do we even know what she's really like? What she'll do to him?"

"No. I've called Children's Services and explained the situation and our concerns. They've agreed to send a social worker over sometime today to check, which is a major concession, because he's not on their caseload."

"And what am I supposed to do with him tomorrow? I don't even know why they were fighting."

"You just let it go. He most likely will. You have to pick your battles with this job."

"Literally. And there are lots of them to pick from."

He smiles at me. I can't find one to give back.

"I also want you to know that I've spoken to the

superintendent, and your principal is being instructed to hire an educational assistant and find you a better space."

"An EA? Not a child and youth worker?"

"No. We don't have the funding right now. You'll be getting an EA who's already in the system. If we get lucky, it'll be someone with experience that will be useful. If not, we'll at least try to make sure there's some training."

"Training? Like I got?" I don't even try to mask the sarcasm.

"Hopefully a lot better. Ideally you both should do the intervention training together. I'll look into it and let you know."

"Okay." I know I should sound more grateful, but I just can't muster up the hypocrisy right now.

"I'll drop by after the boys leave and update you on Donny if you'd like."

"I would appreciate that." This time I do a better job of it because I mean it.

✗

Somehow we three survivors of the fray make it through until home time. I call Cory's house and leave a message about the fight so his mother will know where the lump came from. I don't expect to hear from her. I imagine this is small compared to some of the phone calls she's received in the past.

I'm just hanging up the phone when Mrs. Callahan pops her head in.

"Mr. Norton is back and wants to talk to us about Donny."

He wants to talk to both of us? My stomach does a little pitch.

He's already standing in Mrs. Callahan's office when we walk in. His eyes are grave and my stomach flips the rest of the way over.

"So, things didn't go quite as planned."

"Oh, how so?" Mrs. Callahan asks in what sounds like a less than totally concerned tone. I suspect her stomach is just fine.

"Well, as I told you, I contacted Children's Services, who agreed to send a social worker. I was expecting that to happen later on today, but the worker arrived at the same time as Donny and I did. His mother was already unhappy enough that some board office guy was bringing her son home, and so she basically went off the rails when social services showed up."

"Did she hurt Donny?" My voice comes out smaller and higher than usual.

"Um...no. Actually, she took on the social worker instead. One good hit to the side of the head. Left hook, I think." He smiles a little ruefully, and I bark out a particularly lady-like laugh. Mrs. Callahan looks at both of us with an extremely disapproving stare.

"That must have been interesting for you," I say, trying to sound professional again. Hard to do after impersonating a dog. *Can you impersonate a dog?*

"Well, actually it was pretty hairy. The social worker called the police, and when they arrived, she took Donny into care."

"What?" I'm barking again.

"The social worker wants the mom charged with assault.

She deemed the situation volatile and said that Donny is at risk. She's taking him to a temporary foster home."

"Well, that's wonderful. It will be so much nicer for him than living with that woman." Mrs. Callahan smiles as if we've just heard that Donny is going to Disneyland.

"But he loves his mother. He talks about her all the time. He'll be devastated! It's not like she hurt *him*!" A few hours ago I was the one worrying about sending him home to that woman, and now I'm defending her. If I'm this confused, how must Donny be feeling?

"There's nothing we can do. There'll be an investigation. This isn't the end of it. And I don't know what the truth is about Donny and his mom. Maybe now we'll find out." Norton's voice is grim.

"Well, I think all's well that ends well." Mrs. Callahan is obviously ready to put a lid on this conversation. "Thank you for your help. I think we all need to go home and have a bit of a rest. You'll have your new class and your new EA on Monday." She's obviously saying the last part to me, but she's looking at him and smiling that special smile she saves for people who come from the board office. He's looking at me. I shake my head slightly. It's amazing how quickly things get done around here when Callahan is trying to be impressive.

"They're hoping to find a foster home within range of here so he can continue with you. We'll know more about that next week. He'll likely be away for a day or two."

"Okay thanks, Mr. N," I say, using the boys' diminutive of his name.

"I think we can graduate to a first-name basis by now. It's Daniel, in case you've forgotten." I hope he's kidding and doesn't realize that I actually did forget his name. Daniel is nicer than Norton, I guess.

He smiles at me, and then heads out of the room.

He has a kind smile.

I think I'm going to cry.

CHAPTER 7

Daddy's gone; do you want a troll?

All weekend, images of Donny invade my mind. What is he going through? What must it feel like to suddenly be told you can't be at home with your own mother? That you have to go and stay at a stranger's house until some other stranger tells you what your future holds. To have your whole life turned upside down and inside out in the blink of an eye.

Or the swing of a punch.

All because your teacher wasn't smart enough to figure out how to stop you from swinging your own punch at school.

I wonder about Donny's mother and why she would risk punching a social worker. Is she a bad mom, or was she just angry? Does she hurt Donny or just interfering agents of the system? What would I have done in her position? How would I feel if someone came here to my home and tried to tell me how to raise my children?

I have a sudden image of little girls begging for juice while their mothers ignore them. I try to remember. Did I ever do that with my girls, or did I at least get that part right?

I certainly don't get it all right.

I couldn't even stay married for them, managing instead to sentence them to life in a broken family.

When my Humpty-Dumpty marriage got to the point where so many pieces were missing that it could never be put back together again, I started making plans. Plans are important. They keep life organized and predictable. They give you focus. Setting goals and striving to achieve them form structures out of chaos.

I planned out my divorce as only an A-type personality can. I read—no devoured—every article I could find on the right way to do a divorce. I carefully scrutinized data on custody arrangements, trying to discover which one would have the least impact on my kids. I read everything I could on separation agreements and how to amicably and quickly come to consensus with your former life partner turned adversary. How not to be adversaries at all, so you can have a friendly divorce.

Friendly divorce.

Friendly fire.

I read everything. I thought about everything. I planned everything. I had it all figured out.

Decision number one was that the girls were going to remain living with me full-time. Their dad was going to move out and visit regularly. Consistency is the key to a successful divorce for children. This I know because I heard it on a radio talk show.

Decision number two was that Dad was going to move all of his things out while the girls were at school and daycare so that they didn't have to watch it happen.

Decision number three was that Mommy and Daddy were going to sit down and tell our three-year-old and her seven-year-old sister in simple, compassionate terms why we could no longer live together. Why, even though we loved them more than anything in the world, we still couldn't figure out how to love each other enough to give them a normal family life. Why life didn't work out the way any of us had planned. Why Daddy was going to live in another place and how special that would be because they could visit him there and have two homes. How exciting to have two homes!

I have also told my children, repeatedly, that a large man dressed in red somehow manages to squeeze down our very small chimney every 24th of December and that an equally large rabbit hops around our house once a year throwing chocolate eggs everywhere and that the rule about talking to strangers is suspended every 31st of October, so long as you're dressed in a strange costume and begging for candy.

For years when I was little, I worried about children without chimneys and thought that rabbits laid eggs.

I rehearsed what I was going to say by the hour. "Girls, your daddy and I love you so very much." That's always the opening line. Common sense and pretty much all of the articles I read agree on that one.

"We both love being with you and living here with you more than you will ever know. Mommies and daddies always, always, always love their children." I added all of the "always" myself. Emphasis is important when devastating children.

"Mommies and daddies love each other too, but sometimes they have trouble living together even though they still always, always, always love their children." I read somewhere, many somewheres, that children sometimes blame themselves for their parents' divorce. It's important to reiterate your Mommy-and-Daddy love for them as separate from your grown-up love for each other. Grown-up love is brittle, fragile stuff, easily shattered. Mommy-and-Daddy love is pliable, timeless, and completely indestructible.

Donny's face flashes into my personal history for a second, and I wonder again about his mother. He obviously loves her. Does she love him?

"But even if Mommy and Daddy don't live together anymore, we are both still your parents, and we both love you very, very, very much."

Repetition to reduce the sting.

"Daddy is going to live in a special apartment very close to our house so that he can see you all the time. You'll see him almost as much as you do now. Everything will be fine."

And that fat guy with the beard is going to push a bike down the chimney this year.

✗

It was on a relatively sunny day in April that the final piece of our shattered marital dream finally went missing—a morning that felt relatively normal. Boxes piled in the basement testified otherwise.

On this relatively sunny April morning, the girls and I head off to work and school and daycare just like every other morning. They say good-bye to their dad just like every other morning, not knowing it's the last time that this will happen just this way. Unless I change my mind.

I turn my head, closing my eyes against the tears. This is the right thing to do. I know it is. They can't live in this chaotic, angry household and be okay. This is the right thing to do. It is. I know it is.

Repetition.

I spend my work day in a fog. My mind and body seem mired in emotional quicksand, and I can't force myself to move either one. I sit at my desk and try to look like I'm teaching, but I can barely see the kids. I should have taken the day off, but I somehow just assumed that I would be fine today. He's coming home tonight to have "the talk" and *everyone* is going to be fine.

Except that he just called to tell me he's going to be late. I'm going to have to find a way to keep the girls busy until he gets home so that my oldest won't see that parts of our life are missing. She notices details. I think she's going to be an artist someday.

The day drags to a close, and I sit alone at my desk, trying to figure out what to do now. I can't just pick the girls up and head home.

I'm starting to lose control of the plan.

I sit for another fifteen minutes, then force myself up out of the chair to head over to the daycare. Both girls will be there by now.

"Well, you're nice and early today!" the daycare director says, forcing the cheerfulness through an artificial smile. She knows about us. I told her last week that this was coming, so she could watch the girls, especially my baby, for signs of distress.

"Yes. I guess I am."

"Well, she had a pretty normal day—" she starts. But I interrupt.

"They don't know yet. I guess we're telling them tonight."

"Oh, all right. Thanks for letting me know. I'm so sorry. About everything."

I can't look at her. I know her eyes are brimming with sympathy, and I don't think I can face that right now without curling up on a tiny cot and crying myself into a stupor.

"Thanks." I turn away and head to the pre-school room.

"Mommy! I made you a picture!" She runs to me, sapphire eyes sparkling at me under her mop of blonde curls. This one is going to be a dancer or a singer or something full of life and energy that lives in the spotlight. Not that I plan their lives for them or anything.

"That's wonderful. Let's go get your things and find your sister. I have a surprise for you." *Your father left us today, and now you only have me. Surprise!*

"Hi, Mom." My seven-year-old looks up from her homework and smiles at us when we walk into the "After 4" program room. I don't think I'd assign homework if I taught grade two, but I've never taught anyone that little, so I guess I'm not in a position to judge. But I do it anyway. They're so little! Home time should be playtime. Work should be done at school.

"Hey, sweetie. Grab your stuff. I'm taking you out for supper!"

"Yay!" she says, running out to the coatroom to pack up her bag. I sign her out, and we head to the car.

Driving to McDonald's, the restaurant of choice, I try

to listen to them chatting about their day while internally rehearsing my "Mommy and Daddy are splitting up" speech.

We sit through chicken nuggets and Quarter Pounders. Well, just one Quarter Pounder, which goes into me, even though I'm not hungry. I need protein to face the rest of this day.

"Do you want to go shopping?" I ask, knowing the answer full well.

We head off in great excitement to shop for nothing in particular.

I push the cart down the toy aisle, looking at my beautiful girls and wondering what's going to happen when we get home. How are they going to react? How am I going to react? How am I going to sit there with their father and remember all of the words that I need to say? What if I forget? What if we get into an argument in front of them instead of presenting a united front and everyone starts to cry?

I don't know if I can do it. I can feel the Quarter Pounder dancing around in my gut as panic starts to set in.

"So, girls, I have to tell you something. Daddy and I have decided that he has to live in a different house. He will live near us and still see you, but he won't be at our house every day. We both really love you."

And that's it. All my planning and I puke it out in the toy aisle in a department store.

I didn't say anything that was in my plan at all. One lame "We really love you." No repetition. No real explanation. No father sitting beside me on the couch.

I just did *every*thing wrong.

Perfect end to a perfect day. To an imperfect marriage.

There's a pause as number one processes the information. She looks at the floor for a second and then up at me with the world's biggest, softest, tear-filled eyes. There's a quick flash of something that I can't identify. Sadness? Fear? Panic? Has the damage already begun?

"Okay," she says quietly, nodding her head slightly. She rubs her eyes for a second and then looks at me with a slight smile that makes my heart hurt. "Can we get trolls? The big kind that I saw on TV?"

"I want a troll!" says number two, bouncing excitedly in the shopping-cart seat.

Trolls. They want *trolls*.

Definitely not one of the reactions I had anticipated. Then again, I never planned to break their hearts in the toy department, either.

"Um, sure. Let's check them out." I wheel the cart up and down aisles until we find the big, plastic, ridiculously ugly troll dolls that every recent TV ad has told my children they absolutely must have. The same stupid-looking dolls that I had when I was a kid. We look at a minimum of a dozen before decisions are made and one pink-haired and one turquoise-haired doll are safely placed in the back of our cart.

And that was it.

Parent of the year strikes again.

Daddy's gone; do you want a troll?

CHAPTER 8

Monday, Monday

"Hi. I'm Sean."

"Okay. Hi, Sean." I look up at the young man standing in the doorway of my "new" classroom. New to me, but not to anyone else in this century. Mrs. Callahan has put me down in what we not-so-affectionately call "the Cave." The Cave is a series of classrooms in an old portable that was attached to the school back in the days of overpopulation. The only other class down there is our new group of junior kindergartners. I did question Mrs. Callahan on the wisdom of putting my students across from impressionable three- and four-year-olds, but she didn't have an answer. She did, however, have a time-out room for me.

"And here we have the best part," she says with a flourish, opening the door to what looks like an old office of some description. It's wood-paneled, with an ancient, musty rug on the floor. It smells awful and looks worse.

"The best part?"

"Yes. You mentioned to me that you felt a time-out room was in order. Here you go!"

This is where she wants me to de-escalate frantic children? It would make a better torture chamber. Although, now that I think about it, that could be what Mrs. Callahan had in mind. I can imagine her wistfully remembering the good old days when teaching and parenting were based on the "spare the rod and spoil the child" philosophy.

She has no children of her own. This is likely a very good thing.

She's looking at me expectantly. I think she wants a thank you. I can't find one.

"I'll fix it up a bit and then I'm sure it will be...fine," I manage. She looks mortally offended at my lack of enthusiasm.

"I'll leave you to it then," she says, her false veneer of civility slipping away for the moment. She stalks off down the hall without another word. The kids are coming in about an hour, so I have about fifty-six minutes to set up a classroom that I can teach in.

And now there's this stranger standing in my doorway.

I have no idea what he's doing here. Obviously not a student. At least I hope not, because he looks about twenty.

"I'm your new EA. Mrs. Callahan told me to come on down and introduce myself."

"Oh wow! Really? I completely forgot that I was getting someone. We had kind of a...day...on Friday, and I guess it slipped my mind." Lots of things slipped my mind this weekend. Unfortunately, the one thing that didn't was the endless string of images of what I imagine Donny's face must have looked like as he processed the fact that he's away from his mom. Even if she's a "bad" mom by other people's standards, he doesn't see her that way, and I'm sure he's horrified by the thought of having to live with perfect strangers.

Perfect strangers. Nothing about this situation is perfect.

I can't stop feeling guilty about it. I do know on some kind of intellectual level that it wasn't my fault. I couldn't have known that Donny was going to lose it to such an extreme, and that his mom would do the same. At the moment, I am completely incapable of predicting anything in my classroom. Moods seem to shift with lightning speed. Tension fills the room, but no one will tell me why.

I'm sure that some day I'll know the kids well enough to see it coming. That moment when angry words become violent fists.

Some day. Not today.

I know I couldn't have predicted any of it, but it still feels like my fault on some level.

"So...what do you need me to do?" Sean's voice interrupts my guilt trip, and I look at him blankly. What do I need him to do? How about turning time around so that he's here on Friday instead of today and manages to get to Donny before he loses it on Cory.

"Um, that's a great question. Especially since I forgot all about you." Way to welcome the new staff.

"Well, I'm ready and willing. Mrs. Callahan filled me in a little about the kids, but I don't know very much."

Welcome to the club. Actually, I have learned a little about Donny and Cory since the first day. Both boys have been living with their mothers, and neither of them has a dad in the picture. Mrs. Callahan was kind enough to share her opinion that the single parent "situation," as she calls it, likely is a large contributing factor to the problems the boys have. Mrs. Callahan is a firm believer in the detrimental effects of single parenthood. I swear she looks at me every time she talks about it in a staff meeting.

Cory has an older brother who has been in some trouble with the police. His mother works somewhere downtown. Cory is on medication for ADHD. It's supposed to calm him down. I've spent a fair bit of time perched on a soapbox pleading the evils of drugging children, but I have to admit, I cannot begin to imagine what Cory must be like without his medication. He is ten years old and has gone to nine different schools. From what I can tell so far, he cannot read—at all. No real academic testing has ever been done, because he was never in one school long enough. He kept beating up students and/or staff members to wear out his welcome before anyone could figure out how to teach him.

Donny is also ten years old, almost eleven. He's only been in seven schools. He hasn't assaulted quite as many people, but he's become somewhat of an expert in the area of property damage. Most of his schools decided he was too expensive to keep around.

Donny has no siblings. He and his mom live—lived—up in the low-rent projects over in the next town. His mom doesn't work. There is an unconfirmed suspicion that she occupies her time with drinking and other forms of substance abuse. Donny is also on medication. He doesn't have a diagnosis on record, but I assume someone decided he has ADHD also. Donny talks about his mother a lot. He seems to think she's pretty wonderful.

Cory never talks about his mother or his brother at all.

Neither boy ever talks about a father.

I wonder if my daughters do.

I look up to find Sean looking at me politely, obviously waiting for me to say something. At least one of us has manners. I clear my throat a little and try a little laugh on for size.

"Oh, well, the boys are a handful, I guess. Behavior issues, emotional issues. They like to swear and hit each other and wreck things." *I seriously need to work on my welcome speeches.*

"Cool. Sounds like my weekend job."

"Oh, really?" That sounds promising.

"Yep. I'm actually not an EA, even though they're calling me one. I hope that's not a problem. I just finished school, and I couldn't find a full-time job, so I've been working part-time at a group home for kids with all kinds of problems, and I've had some crisis intervention training there. Not a lot, but enough to know what to do if a kid does a freak out. My mom works with a guy from your board office, and he called her and asked if I was available. I think they were supposed to move someone here from another school, but no one was available. So here I am."

I look at him with the same level of appreciation I feel for a large chocolate sundae after a long week at work.

Sounds like someone might have pulled a string or two for me. Since I'm just looking at him and forgetting to talk again, he decides to take another turn.

"Anyway, I'm no expert or anything, but the boys at the home are pretty intense, so there's not much I haven't seen."

"That's...great. I need all the help I can get."

"Looks like you're moving in. Is there more stuff to bring in?" He looks around the sparsely furnished, blank-walled room. The floor is cracked in a dozen places, and the walls are some kind of strange-looking painted brick that make it feel institutionalized somehow. There aren't any shelves. There are about ten sad-looking desks sitting forlornly in a scatter pattern across the room.

"Yes. Pretty much everything! Here, I'll show you where it all is."

And that was that. Sean somehow roped our custodian into helping—something I hadn't even thought of—and the two men had everything moved into my room within about thirty minutes. Sean got to work putting up the few wall decorations we had in our half room, and I tried to find some work for the boys to begin their day with, so that we would have some kind of normalcy to start what is going to be anything but a "normal" day.

Donny hasn't arrived by the time the cabs drop off the other two. No one has contacted me about him at all, so I have no idea where he is or when he might be coming back—if ever.

Cory and Kevin fly out the doors of their respective cabs and run up to me. If I didn't know better, I might think they're excited to see me.

"So, is Donny still in trouble? My mom said you shoulda called the cops on account of my head having a big lump on it. She said I shoulda hit him back, teach him a lesson. Did you call the cops? Is he going to a new school now?" Cory shoots the questions at me in rapid succession.

He's bouncing up and down, his eyes practically spinning in their sockets. Kevin is watching him with great interest. He isn't bouncing up and down, but Baby is. She's being thrown straight up in the air, spiraling down with the grace of an Olympic diver on every toss.

Sean is standing a few feet behind me, and Cory stops talking long enough to notice him.

"What the fuck you staring at? Who the fuck are you anyway?" He steps toward Sean in what I assume he thinks is a menacing manner. He's only about four feet two and about seventy pounds soaking wet, which doesn't seem to faze the six-foot-ish Sean at all.

"I'm Sean. Who are you?"

"Why do you care?"

"Well, I'm going to be working in your classroom, and it's probably easier to do that if I know who you are." His voice is calm and easy. He seems like a natural with them. Cory is still moving constantly, weaving and dodging like a pint-size prize fighter.

"This the A-hole you told us about?" He turns to glare at me.

"Well, actually, I said 'EA' not 'A-hole,' but yes, this is the…person."

"It's a guy." He sounds so surprised that I have to smile. I had been expecting a woman too, as it seems that most EAs in our area are female. I'm surprised that Cory cares, though.

"Thanks for noticing, bud," Sean says with a grin.

"My name is Cory, A-hole, not bud!"

"Thanks for telling me. My name is Sean, not A-hole. Cory is a cool name." Cory stops bouncing for a split second, his eyes telling me that he's wondering if he's being made fun of. He looks at Sean as if he's going to try on his mother's advice about punching people. Then he relaxes his face and almost smiles.

"Yeah, it is. This is Kevin. Kevin, this guy is Sean. New teacher dude or whatever." He turns to look at Kevin, who's still teaching Baby new aerial maneuvers.

"Dickhead," says Kevin.

"This is Baby," says Cory, apparently now in charge of social introductions.

Sean watches the whale spiral down into Kevin's out-stretched hands. He looks over at me for a second, eyebrows raised. I shrug my shoulders and grin. He smiles back and then taps the whale gently on the head.

"Hi, Baby. Nice to meet you."

"Hi, Sean," says Baby, doing a final, death-defying leap up into the stratosphere before we all trudge down to our new room.

Our day starts out relatively smoothly. Seeing as the ratio is currently one-to-one, this should not be surprising. On the other hand, after about an hour of nonstop, virtually hysterical-level motion from Cory, it finally occurs to me that he might have missed his morning meds. A phone call to his mother at work is not very helpful. She can't remember if he had them or not because she was "too busy getting ready for work to keep track of his problems."

We can't risk double dosing, so basically Sean has to chase

Cory around until noon finally arrives and we can safely give him his "at school" dose.

After an almost-calm afternoon, punctuated by only a few verbal outbursts from Cory and Baby, the boys go home, and I leave Sean doing a bit of tidying up while I search out a free phone line to call Daniel to see what's going on with Donny.

"He's in a foster home, but it's about ninety minutes away. We're trying to figure out how to finance a cab for that distance," he tells me when I finally get him on the line.

"He's going to travel ninety minutes each way? Three hours on the road and six hours here? Does that make sense?"

"More sense than putting him in a school without resources where he's sure to fail. Again. Add in the fact that we have no idea how long he's even going to be in this home, and it seems that his best chance is coming back to you."

"Is he likely to go home to his mother ever again?" I can hear the guilt in my voice. Rationally, I know that his home might not be the best place for him, but I still feel like I ripped a family apart.

"Likely? It depends on a lot. How far the social worker takes the assault-charge threat. Whether the investigation shows any sort of abuse toward Donny. It's not a quick or easy thing to take a kid away permanently. There's generally a lot of back and forth before that happens."

"And in the meantime, the kid doesn't know where he belongs anymore."

"Well, at least he'll still be with you at the school, once I get things fixed up. He needs some consistency in his life right now."

"I guess. I've sure been a lot of help to him so far." The self-pity is just oozing into the little holes in the phone— probably dripping down all over him.

"I'll keep in touch and let you know when he's coming back. You got your new room and Sean today?"

"Yes, thank you. He seems like a good kid."

"He is. He's young and not exactly fully trained, but he does have a bit of experience, and I don't think he's easily shaken. I think he'll be good for the boys."

"Yeah, well, he still has more training than I do. He might be able to teach me a few things." *I seriously have to stop this. I'm going to drown him.*

"Talk to you soon." He hangs up before I can say good- bye. Probably going to get a towel.

I close my eyes, thinking about all the kids like Donny, moving from house to house, family to family, school to school. Never feeling like they're at home. What kind of life is that for a child? The one thing a child should be able to count on is that there is this place called home that will always be there, filled with unconditional love.

I've been fighting like a she-bear for the right to hold on to the family home in my separation-slash-divorce. I feel like my daughters will feel safer and less like the whole founda- tion of their lives has shaken loose if the actual foundation they're used to stays underneath their feet.

I know that a home is more than four walls and a roof. I know that it's the people inside that make it a home. I'm sure I read that somewhere on a greeting card.

I know my girls would feel safe and loved anywhere that they ended up living with me, but I am totally obsessed with needing to stay put. I don't want the girls to have to pack up their bedrooms that I spent so much time decorating just for them. I can't face the sight of little pink teddy bears and plastic horses disappearing into cardboard boxes while two pairs of blue eyes look at me tearfully.

I think it will all be easier for them if we can just stay in our home. More normal. Safer.

How does a child feel when he suddenly can't be at home anymore? When everything he's used to is suddenly gone? When strangers decide he will be safer living somewhere he's never been before, where the walls and the roof are as different as the people inside it?

Does he feel safe?

Or just lost.

CHAPTER 9

Very small victories

"He does what?"

"Foams at the mouth when he's mad. And he's freakishly strong for his size. Almost impossible to restrain. At least that's what the other school tells me. I'm sure it will be different here."

"Why?"

"Why what?"

"Why would it be different here?"

"Well, he will be in a special class now."

"Oh. Right." *An instant cure. Obvious to anyone who walks past our classroom and hears the dulcet sounds of young boys swearing.*

A special class. Which isn't actually a class at all. Which, at the moment, consists of two students, because Donny is still not back. While I'm not surprised that my numbers are going up, pushing us past the one-to-one ratio that I am growing to really like, I did want Donny back in and settled with Sean and the new room before there were any more changes. I tried to explain this to Mrs. Callahan when she arrived in my room first thing this morning to inform me that she has a new student on the hook.

"Well, I don't think that's going to work out for you," she said, followed by that insincere smile again. "The family is actually waiting in my office. I've already explained everything to them."

I wonder if she waits until the last minute to tell me so that I don't have time to protest properly or to get my consultant involved in the process.

It's only paranoia if no one is actually out to get you.

"Explained everything? Explained what?"

"Oh, lots of things. All about you and Sean and your new room and the new time-out room. How things are different here than in his other schools. Better staff-student ratio, no suspensions for inappropriate behavior—"

"What? What do you mean?"

"Well, I mean that the students' issues will be dealt with here. At school. Now that you have Sean and the two rooms, there is no reason to be sending them home. More parents will be interested in bringing their children here if they know that."

"I think that's kind of a dangerous promise to make. I mean, these guys are capable of a lot." Not to mention the little fact that no one talked to me about it first.

Definitely not paranoia. This is real. I think she hates me.

It's not that I've ever been a big fan of suspensions…now I'm even less so, after the Donny mess. But at the same time, my students don't have much in the way of internal boundary systems. There has to be something in place for those times when it's just too dangerous for them to be here.

When *they're* just too dangerous to be here.

"Oh, I'm sure you'll be fine."

I open my mouth to finish my protest, but we're already in the office.

Mrs. Callahan's office is actually a pretty nice place. It's air-conditioned in the summer and heated in the winter. It has chairs that are soft, so that parents are lulled into a sense of complacency by the comfort. She has pretty pictures on the wall and pretty candies in a dish. I'm sure the Williams family is under the illusion that my classroom looks just like this.

Mrs. Callahan introduces us, and both parents smile at me. Their son, Mike, does not.

"Well, I'm happy to meet you. I can tell you, I'm tired of schools calling me to pick him up just because they can't deal with him. I'm glad they have a nice place like this one where he'll actually get to stay at school and learn something." Mr. Williams nods at me, agreeing with himself. I do my best to smile.

"Well, we'll do our best. Hopefully Mike will find this to be a nice place." The words seem lame. I look over at Mike. He shakes his head slightly, lip curled up into the suggestion of a sneer. *Definitely lame.*

He is not foaming at the mouth right now. He's sizing me up, squinting at me appraisingly through a pair of bright blue eyes set in a round, soft face topped off by a crown of golden blond hair. I would have thought him angelic-looking except for the shrewdly assessing gaze that is currently making me feel a little squirmy. I try to match him, squinting right back, but he's good. I'm being outmatched by a nine-year-old, and he's only been here thirty seconds.

This should be fun.

I call down and ask Sean to pick up the other guys. Much as I am still hoping that Donny is coming back, I am really praying it isn't today.

"Okay, Mike. Follow me, and we'll get started." Started at what? I have no file. No information other than that he foams at the mouth.

"Bye, Mikey!" his mom calls after us. This kid does not look like a Mikey to me. He obviously agrees, because he doesn't even look at her.

He follows me silently, walking into the room behind me. Sean has the other two relatively settled by the time we get there. I'm really hoping neither of them figures out a way to set Mike off so we can see if the other school is telling the truth.

Cory stares at him. Kevin looks up and decides it's his job to be the welcoming committee.

"Dickhead."

"Shut your mouth, fuck-face," Mike says, without any inflection in his voice at all. I wait for the fireworks to go off. There's no way Cory is going to let some new kid get away with that.

Mike walks over to the desk I point out to him and sits down, completely ignoring Sean and the boys. Cory doesn't say a word. It's almost like he's afraid, as if Mike's some kind of mob boss who just walked in on a couple of his underlings slacking off on the job.

I have a bad feeling about this.

The first half of the day is pretty calm. Mike doesn't actually do any work, but we aren't going to push that too much in the first half of his first day. We'll save that for the second half.

Recess arrives, our version of it anyway. We don't do recess with the rest of the school yet. It is a goal, but at the moment, the total lack of structure and the presence of all the other kids in the school are too overwhelming for my students. Almost without exception, my boys have long histories of serious schoolyard incidents that have resulted in recesses being spent in the office. By the time they get to me, I think they've actually forgotten how to play outside, if they ever knew in the first place. We go out by ourselves and practice different sports and schoolyard games so that they'll be ready when the time comes to reintegrate into the regular population.

Well, mostly at this point in time, we have them practice not kicking the crap out of each other. Today we're attempting two-on-two soccer, and the focus is on kicking the ball instead of the leg of the person running beside you.

Mike mostly watches from the sidelines. We give him the day to observe. I hope he isn't plotting a military coup.

"Okay, guys, time's up. Cory, don't bother!" He's aiming the ball at Kevin's head.

"Just kidding. I would never hurt Kev. Right bud?" Cory throws the ball at Sean instead. Sean snags it and heads toward the school, Kevin and Cory following him without argument for a change.

Mike follows along behind, stopping at the bottom of the wheelchair ramp that no one but us ever uses. He turns around, staring back out at the schoolyard, refusing to look at me.

"I'm staying out," he says, in that same atonal voice he used on Kevin in the classroom.

"No, you're not. It's time to come in."

Mike stands at the bottom of the ramp and looks directly at me. I try to stare him down calmly, telling myself not to flinch under his gaze. Pretty sure I now know what a deer feels like when a wolf shows up wanting lunch.

"I'm not going in. I like it outside."

"You don't have a choice." I look at Sean, who has stopped at the door. He ushers the other two in ahead of him and does his best to block their view. They're peering around him, excited to check out the new-guy drama presentation.

Mike is standing his ground, trying us on for size to see if we fit as badly as the suits of authority in his other schools. Checking to see how far he can go and what we're going to do about it that's different.

"Yes I do. I choose to stay outside." His voice never changes, and he never makes eye contact. There's no emotion in evidence at all.

"It's time to come in. You can't stay outside alone. It's a safety issue. You need to come in. Now." I'm standing in front of him while Sean watches for a second. I see him duck inside, leaving me here alone.

"I'm not coming in. You can't make me come in. I can

go wherever I want whenever I want. You can't fucking touch me." He turns around as if to head back onto the ramp so he can get off to the side and avoid me in his bid for freedom, but he comes up short. Sean is standing in his way.

"Ms. Jackson has the boys." I guess she sent her kids back to their classrooms so she could guard mine, even though it isn't lunchtime. Teamwork.

"Actually, we can. We don't want to, but we will if we feel it's necessary for your safety. Your parents signed up for that when they placed you with us." I'm behind him talking, and he doesn't acknowledge me, but I know he's listening.

"My parents would never sign anything like that. They don't let anyone touch me. I do what I want. When I want." He hasn't moved or raised his voice. His body is tense, vibrating with what I assume is suppressed emotions.

"Not here. Here you do what we want you to do, when we want you to do it." Sean is calm and appropriate. Mature and adult. In control.

"Move." Mike is calm and inappropriate. Mature and adult. In control.

"Nope. You need to go back up the ramp into the school. Now!" The words sound more juvenile and challenging than I intend. What is it about this kid?

"Move." Mike's tone changes, just a little. I feel a little plunge of dread in my stomach. It's not physical fear exactly. This is a kid, after all. Sean is three of him. I'm at least two. That makes five.

But I hate this. I don't want to get physical with a student. I want someone else to do it.

Actually, I don't want anyone to have to do it.

"Come on. Let's head back in. It'll be home time soon." Sean is still cool. He's really proving to be a natural at dealing with these kids. Mike continues to stand perfectly still, but I see his hands slowly curling into fists. I gesture a warning to Sean—a millisecond too late. Mike suddenly springs into action. Literally. It's like he's some kind of robot kid with special springs in his feet that propel him upward, moving him and his fists up into Sean's face in a fraction of a second. Before he can take another swing, Sean has both his hands and has spun him around into a restraint.

Mike kicks and growls, fiercely twisting his body back and forth, trying to bite the hands that are holding him. He spits in my face as I try to get around behind him to help Sean with the hold.

Five times his body weight, and we're losing him.

"Hi. I happened to be in the school, and Mrs. Callahan mentioned there might be a problem."

I don't bother looking up at the sound of Daniel's voice. *Might be a problem? Does he have eyes?*

Daniel comes around the other side and tries to get a good hold. Mike's moving so fast and so ferociously that none of us can even begin to figure out what's going on and who should be holding which body part. He's making inhuman sounds that seem to be coming from a place so deep inside of him that we'll never be able to reach down and find it.

"Look!" The word pops out of Sean's mouth before he can stop it. He gestures with his head toward Mike's face. White, foamy spittle is pouring out of Mike's mouth and dripping down onto his carefully pressed first-day-of-school shirt. Sean shakes his head a little, and the expression in his eyes tells me that this is something he hasn't seen at the group home. Daniel doesn't look very confident either. I'm pretty sure none of us knows what we're supposed to do right now.

"Mike, you have to try to calm down. Come on, buddy, you need to get through this and come inside." I have to look past the foam and try to find the little boy. He seems to have disappeared.

He's beyond words at this point, and the only sounds are strange guttural growls and a wet, slurping sound as water pours from his mouth. We're simultaneously afraid to hold on and afraid to let go. Restraining the kids is the worst part of this job, and we do everything we can to avoid it. Once you have them in a restraint, it's sometimes incredibly difficult to figure out when it's safe to let go.

We're looking at each other, trying to read faces and figure out what's best for him and for us when suddenly, he just slumps down to the ground. Sean goes down with him as Daniel and I let go gently. Sean loosens his grip, just a little. They sit like that for a few moments, tied up together in an awkward parody of a hug.

"I'll go in now," Mike says in a quiet voice.

We look at each other, and I shake my head slightly. It's a small victory. A very small one.

We walk up the ramp in single file, Sean bringing up the rear. We're all drained, emotionally and physically.

Just as we get inside the building, Mike turns around and punches Sean full force in the stomach.

"No one fucking touches me!" he screams, as Sean grabs him again. He's unbelievably back into full-out "blow" mode, kicking, screaming, and punching as if he had all the energy in the world.

This time, he's made the mistake of pitching his battle right outside the time-out room. We haven't used it yet, but if ever there was someone in need of de-escalation, it's this one. He's finally starting to tire by now, the initial burst of frantic strength weakening enough that the three of us are able to quickly and efficiently put him in the room and close the door. We watch through the safety glass window as he has another energy surge and starts to kick and punch the walls. He's yelling at us to get his father.

This is all wrong. The time-out room is supposed to be a place to help them, not lock them in. But I don't think any one of us would be safe going in there with him right now.

"Mike, you need to calm down and listen to me. We need to go over some of the rules of this school. You need to calm down so we know it's okay to come in."

"Fuck you!"

"All right, I'll try again in a few minutes. When you're able to calm down enough to talk to me, I'll be ready to listen to you."

"Are you two all right with him now? Or do you want me to stay and speak with his parents?" Daniel asks. I look at him for a second, tempted beyond measure to just hand it all over to him.

"No. It's best if I handle the rest myself. My class. My authority and all that. But thanks. Glad you showed up when you did."

"Glad I could help. I'll let Mrs. Callahan know what's going on, and I'll check in tomorrow."

I leave Sean guarding the door, watching to make sure Mike doesn't actually hurt himself, and head back to the classroom. The day is almost over, and I want to get our other boys back and out the door without any more major upsets.

They're doing much better than I expected with a complete stranger watching over them. The intensity of Mike's first day seems to have shaken them a little, and they're both sitting in their seats pretending to read.

"Good job, guys. Thanks for making this a little easier."

"What's his problem?" Cory asks.

"Dickhead," says Kevin.

"Oh, right," says Cory.

A laugh spurts out of me before I can stop it. Both boys look at me as if I'm nuts.

"Anyway, guys. It's just...everyone has a bad day sometimes. Especially when they're somewhere new. Right?"

"Whatever." Empathy isn't Cory's best trick.

"Well, let's get organized so you don't miss your rides."

They're both more than happy to comply. Today, anyway.

Mike's parents haven't arranged transportation as yet, and no one has called from the office to say that they're here to pick him up, so we have a few minutes. I head back down to the time-out room.

Sean is still standing, watching through the window. Mike has stopped kicking and screaming for the moment.

"Hi, Mike. Are you ready to talk a bit?"

"Fuck you, bitch!"

"Guess not. Okay, well, I'll just let your parents know that you're going to be a little late getting down to the office to go home. When I get back, we'll talk a little and make sure you understand what happened here before you head off."

"I want my parents here right now. I'm going home now! You can't keep me here!"

I walk away and down to the other end of the school where the lights are brighter and the air smells fresher. Mike's parents are waiting in the front office.

"How was his afternoon?" his dad asks as I walk in.

"Well, he started off all right, but things got a little tougher after recess. He's still in time out and will need a few minutes of de-escalation before he can go home."

"Well, we're here now, so we can come down and get him and take him home. I can manage him."

"Unfortunately, that won't work. Most of the time, we're going to be dealing with a cab company, and we won't be able to send him home in an agitated condition. He has to learn how to calm down and follow directions—our directions—if he's going to be safe."

"I really think it's best if I just go down and talk to him. He'll come with me."

"I have no doubt about that at all. He wants to go with you to get away from me. But that's not in his best interest."

"Hello, Mr. and Mrs. Williams. You're here to get Mike." Stating the obvious, Mrs. Callahan arrives on the scene, high heels clicking, perfume wafting, and blood-red manicured nails extended in a girlie handshake. Mr. Williams ignores her hand and her perfume.

"We're trying to, but she has him down in that time-out room, and she won't let us take him." He points to me. Mrs. Callahan looks at me like she wishes she could put me in the time-out room. Permanently.

"What's this about, Ms. S?" she asks, all false politeness over an undertone of steely anger.

"It's about authority. Mine. He has to know that I'm in

charge here. That he has to do what I ask him to. Which is simply to talk to me for a few moments about what happened."

"He had one of his tempers?" There's an almost imperceptible note of pride in the father's voice. Almost.

"I'm not sure that's the best or most descriptive term for it, but yes, he had a significant episode. He's in the time-out room, under supervision, and he needs to talk with me before he can go."

"He can talk to you tomorrow."

"He won't be welcome back into my class tomorrow if you take him without letting me follow through." I look at Callahan, just daring her to fight me on this one. She opens her mouth as if to do exactly that, but I see the quick calculations in her eyes as she figures it out. She knows. No one else will take my class. She'll be the one stuck trying to find supply teachers to take care of things if I suddenly get a doctor's note saying the stress is too much for me and that I need to go back to my old job.

Mr. Williams looks at me with the same blue eyes that stared at me out of Mike's face. Emotions flicker across them quickly. I think I see anger and frustration and a few others that go by too quickly to recognize. Finally I see resignation.

"Okay. I guess we can wait a few minutes."

I head back down.

"Mike, I just spoke with your dad. He's waiting up in the office and will come and get you as soon as we've had our talk. So you just let me know when you're ready."

"Are you fucking kidding me? Go get my dad now. You can't keep me here. Get my dad. Now, bitch!"

"I see you're not ready. I'll just wait out here until you are."

"Now! Get my dad now! You stupid, fucking bitch!"

Two hours and about two hundred "stupid fucking bitches" later, he finally decides it's time to talk.

Mostly he just ran out of steam. But he sits quietly and pretends to listen to me as I babble away about self-control and first days and other random things, then he walks quietly to the office where his father is still waiting.

Obviously Mike's father has run out of schools, or I don't think he would have given in to me.

It's a small victory.

A very small one.

CHAPTER 10

Changes

"Donny is coming back today. I got the call last night. I have no idea what condition he'll be in or how the other guys will react, so just be ready for anything."

Sean looks up from the work he's doing on the time-out room. It's about a week after Mike christened it with a few new cracks in the wall and rips in the carpet. We decided if it's going to be a room that helps kids calm down, it shouldn't look like a room where criminals are questioned by large, scary-looking secret agents. Sean found a couple of relatively comfortable chairs that aren't very throw-able. Right now he's putting up a couple of posters—high up—that were being recycled from his group home. Trying to make isolation look more homey.

"Okay. We had a pretty good day yesterday, so maybe they'll come in a good mood."

"Wouldn't it be nice if it was all that predictable?" I laugh with him. Every morning brings a brand new day here, from what I can see. Not much carryover from one day to the next. How they start their days likely has a lot more to do with what happened between leaving here and coming back than anything else. And I have no idea what that is. I can't imagine their home lives, even though I've tried.

I might get a bit of a window into Mike's life soon, though. Apparently, there was an incident at home that prompted a neighbor to call Children's Services. A social worker has paid a visit and is going to come to the school to share a little bit of insight with us. If he's discovered any, that is. Mike's parents are pretty convinced that he only "misbehaves" at school and that the neighbor was either overreacting or flat-out lying. *Can you say denial?*

I head down to the pick-up area. Donny's cab is coming first, which makes no sense to me at all. He lives the farthest away by a long shot, and he's going to be arriving a full ten minutes before the other guys. The poor kid has to get his life in order ten minutes earlier to come to school. One change after another. And it's only just beginning.

I get there just as his van pulls up. The door opens, and he steps out. He looks different. I'm not sure what it is at first.

"Hi, Ms. S," he says.

"Hi, Donny. Glad you're back." He nods. Did he get a haircut? No, that's not it. What is it?

"I don't live with my mom anymore." He blurts it out at me. He looks surprised that he said it out loud.

"I know. I'm sorry to hear it." I look at him again. I know what it is. He's clean. His face is scrubbed, and his hair shines a little in the morning light. His hands aren't gray, and his fingernails aren't black. He doesn't look like an unkempt little waif anymore. Now he looks…kempt.

But not very happy.

"I live with Maggie and Steve. They're old, and they live about a gazillion miles from here. From anywhere."

"I hear they're nice." I'm making it up. I shouldn't do that, but I can't think of anything else to say.

"They're okay, I guess. They're not mean. Not exactly nice either. Just not…anything."

"Well, let's get you settled back into the classroom before anyone else comes. There've been a few changes since you left that I need to tell you about." Changing the subject because I can't think of anything remotely helpful to say.

His eyes fly up to meet mine, and the panic in them at the thought of something else in his life changing breaks my heart.

"It's okay. It's nothing too drastic." Just a new classroom, new staff person, and new classmate. Basically new everything. Except me. And Cory. And Kevin. Oh, and Baby. That should be a comfort to him.

I take him down and show him everything. Sean is cool as usual. Donny is wary and keeps his distance. He looks around the room, and his eyes rest on the poster he'd brought in the day after he became one of my students. He looks pleased for a second. Almost as pleased as I was that second day when I saw that it was a nice, appropriate picture of Harry Potter flying on a broom.

"This my desk?" he asks.

"Yes. You're beside Kevin. I thought that way you could help him with things."

He nods, and I silently congratulate myself on my wise choice of seating arrangement.

The other three arrive relatively calmly. Mike completely ignores Donny when he sees him. Kevin looks at him briefly.

"Dickhead."

We really have to work on his vocabulary. Maybe Baby can help.

"Hey Kev," Donny says and flashes him the briefest of smiles.

"You're back," Cory says, always observant.

"Yeah."

"Did they put you in jail? On account of smashing me in the head?" Cory rubs his head, which is long-since bump-less.

"No. Just a foster home." Judging from his tone, to Donny the two things are pretty much equal. I take a second to wonder if he really believes that his punch is the one that put him in foster care. Didn't anyone explain it to him?

The morning is strangely—eerily—easy. Donny is unnaturally calm. So much so that I start to wonder if they've overmedicated him at the new home or something. Not that calm is bad. But he's slowed down to the point of being almost immobile.

Mike is working at being disinterested, and the effort of deliberately ignoring Donny keeps him quiet for a change. His day-one blowup hasn't been repeated, but he has a mouth on him, and he uses it to escalate Cory on a daily basis. He's sneaky about it and smart. He knows exactly what to say and when to say it for maximum impact and minimum adult detection.

Kevin is never very loud. He's mostly passive resistant so far. Very good at doing nothing. Then again, I haven't tried to make him wear sleeves yet.

By the time one o'clock rolls around, I start thinking that this might be quite the anomaly—a whole day with no exploding children in it.

By the time one fifteen rolls around, things have changed—with a vengeance.

"What did you fucking say to me?" Donny flies up out of his seat with the force of a cannonball escaping. He lands directly beside Mike's desk. Sean is over there in a split second, but Donny already has the front of Mike's shirt bunched up in his hand.

"Nothing freak. You must be, like, hallucinating or something." Mike smirks at him and grabs Donny's wrist, twisting it hard enough to make him let go. Sean puts his hand very lightly on Mike's arm.

"Let go, Mike," he says calmly. Mike glares at him. He's made it clear he doesn't like to be touched. We've made it clear that we won't touch him if he doesn't give us a reason to.

He drops Donny's wrist, and I try to stifle the sound of my sigh of relief.

Sean is still looking at Mike, watching his face for signs that will tell him which way this situation is going to go. And that's why he misses the look on Donny's face just before he takes a swing and makes contact with Mike's cheek.

"You stupid, fucking asshole. You don't say anything about my mom!" Donny screams, while Sean switches gears and gets him into a restraint.

"What mom is that? The stupid bitch who sent you to a

retard home?" Mike laughs at him. I haven't seen him laugh before. It's not like any laughter I've ever heard. It's a cold sound, an icy wind whipping into the room, making me shiver.

"Mike, that's enough." I'm standing beside him, as Sean tries to move Donny away from the desk.

"*Mike* that's enough? You're seriously fucking kidding me, right? He hit me! And I didn't even hit the freak-faced faggot back. And you're giving *me* shit?"

"He called my mom a whore!" Donny screams, kicking backward at Sean. They're slowly moving toward the door, folded together in a gyrating mess of body parts, a bizarre parody of a dance move sliding across the floor.

"Hey, I'm just telling the truth man!" Mike calls out.

"Shut up, fuckhead," Cory decides to join in. I would rather he didn't.

"Both of you be quiet!" I try to keep my voice calm as I raise the volume. "Cory, I would appreciate it if you would just help Kevin with his math. And Mike, that's enough out of you. Donny had no right to hit you, but I need you to stop this. Now."

Cory opens his mouth and then changes his mind and goes over to sit with Kevin. I'm pretty sure neither of them is planning on doing math, but at the moment, I really don't care.

Sean and Donny are heading out the door. Donny is crying now. I know that Cory slows down the physical acting out once the tears start to flow, and I'm hoping the same thing is happening right now with Donny. Sean has switched his hold, escorting Donny to our newly decorated time-out room with one arm firmly holding his shoulder, ready to switch back if he starts to escalate again.

I stand in the doorway to watch their progress. I look across the hall and shake my head as a pair of solemn brown eyes stares up at me from about three feet off the floor.

"Go back into your room, honey. Go find your teacher," I say to the tiny junior kindergarten student who will most likely have nightmares for a week. The eyes widen a bit, probably in fear, because I'm pretty sure they all think I'm some sort of evil witch lording it over a dark and dusty lair filled with loud-mouthed, profanity-spewing monsters. She looks at me for another second and then disappears back into the safe haven of the bright and colorful land of crayons and circle time.

I turn back to the classroom. Mike seems to have forgotten the whole incident. He's staring down at a book, doing a reasonable facsimile of reading. Cory is laughing as Kevin makes Baby dance across the top of his desk. I know I should go and talk to Mike about what he said to Donny, but I don't want to escalate the situation again. I want to keep things calm long enough to have a chance to talk to Donny.

I've never seen him cry before. I've seen him scream and yell and kick and punch. But never cry.

"Ms. S?" I turn back to the hallway at the sound of my name. Sean is standing at the door of the time-out room.

"Yes?"

"Donny would like to talk to you. He's pretty upset. Can we switch?"

I look back at the kids. Still calm enough. I shouldn't really leave Sean with three students. Technically, an EA should not be left alone with groups. The time-out room should really be attached to my classroom, but this arrangement is the only one I've got, so we have to make do. Which means bending the rules—all the way until they break.

"Okay." I feel like calling out "one, two, three—go!" as we dash down the hall, trying to make it seem like no one has been left alone.

Donny is still crying. No, more than crying. Sobbing, great big hiccupping sobs accompanied by a flood of tears as his nose runs into his mouth. I dig through my pockets looking for a tissue. I manage to find a restaurant napkin, which will have to do. I hand it to him. He looks at it like he has no idea what I want him to do with it.

"For your nose," I say, gesturing toward his face as if I'm not sure he knows where his body parts are. Maybe a rousing chorus of "Head and Shoulders, Knees and Toes" would cheer him up.

He wipes his nose, smearing the mess across his face. He looks at me with anguished eyes, and it occurs to me that cleanliness is not the issue here.

"Donny? You aren't this upset about Mike, are you?"

"No. He's just an asshole."

"This is about your mom?" *Brilliant deduction, Professor Holmes.*

"Yes." He starts to cry harder—if that's even possible.

"Oh, honey. You have to calm down."

"It's too late! I already blew it!"

"No. This wasn't your fault. The fight with Cory isn't the reason you went to the foster home." I'm getting out of my depth here. Again. I don't know what to say to him.

"No, not that! Today! I blew it today!"

"What do you mean?"

"I blew my visit with my mom! I'm supposed to see her Saturday, and now I can't!" He starts to wail at the top of his lungs. The little ones next door are getting an earful. Their teacher, Sharon, told me they call the sounds coming from here "the boogeyman in the closet." She's tried to explain, but the reality is actually worse than the fantasy, so none of us has figured out what to do about it.

"I don't understand." I don't feel very helpful right now. I really don't get what he's saying.

"My social bitch Melanie said that if I messed up at school, I couldn't go see my mom."

"Your social *worker* said that?" Emphasis on the "worker"—everything's a social-skills lesson. Although maybe his word is more accurate.

Did she really tell the kid that his whole life hinges on how he behaves at school? That the payoff for being a good boy is something as astronomically important as spending time with his mother? That won't stress him out at all. Nothing like a little incentive to cure an emotionally disturbed kid and make him a model student.

One thing anyone working with these kids figures out quickly is that making the stakes too high generally results in creating an impossible situation. These children find positive reinforcement just as hard to deal with as the negative. Actually, harder most of the time. Their self-control is so fragile that setting wonderful, and distant, goals for them basically sets them up for disaster.

If I've figured it out, a social worker who does this

full-time would have to know it. What the hell was she think-ing? This is ridiculous. I can't see it working with any kid, let alone one of my students. It would be like telling my daughter that she can only go see her dad on the weekend if she passes her math test. She'd be so uptight, she'd probably forget how to count to ten.

"Ye-e-e-s!" The word is one long gulping sob.

"Well, you can stop crying because I have no intention of telling your social worker about today. It's your first day back. You have a lot to deal with." Like losing your whole entire world in one single moment. And being told that you can keep on losing it over and over again every time you have a bad day—when you're in a class for kids who can't seem to stop having bad days.

What the *hell* was she thinking?

It's time to have a talk with the social bitch.

CHAPTER 11

Social skills

I have the greatest respect for social workers. It's a desperately tough job. It's hard enough to deal with children from troubled homes at school, but it's immeasurably harder to be the one who actually has to walk into those homes. The one who has to make life-altering decisions every day. The one who is constantly confronted with the most desperate of human nature within a system where there are never enough people or resources to get the job done.

All social workers are not created equal, however. Just like teachers—and every other profession out there—there are great ones, good ones, mediocre ones, and then there are those who should be looking for another line of work. Luckily, I've met very few of the latter. I'm afraid that Donny's new worker might be one of the few.

I'm not exactly sure of the protocol here, so I call Daniel and explain the situation.

"I wouldn't worry about it too much. I'm sorry Donny got upset, but it sounds to me like someone who's just trying too hard and maybe doesn't have a lot of experience with the whole school versus home relationship. I'll give her a call and politely explain it to her from the school's point of view and make sure she talks to Donny."

That's diplomatic of him. Guess that's why he's the board office guy and I'm teaching in the Cave.

I would have called and said, "Hey listen, social bitch, back off my kid."

Well, not really, but I wanted to. My she-bear instincts come out with my students the same way they do with my own children sometimes, and I strike out first and think later.

Sounds like a few young boys I know.

"Okay. Just make sure she tells him that nothing he does at school will screw up his home visits. I already told him that, but he really needs to hear it from her too."

"Will do. Talk to you later."

As I hang up the phone, Mrs. Callahan pops her head in and reminds me that another social worker is waiting for me. Mike's this time.

Social workers, teachers, doctors, parents, principals—so many adults in the lives of these kids. It reminds me of an old joke: how many adults does it take to screw up a kid?

Too many cooks throwing random stuff into the frying pan with no consistency at all, making a total mess of these kids' lives. Everyone expecting different things from them and telling them different stories until they literally don't know if they're coming or going.

It's amazing that they survive at all.

I walk into Mrs. Callahan's super cozy office and shake hands as I'm introduced to Steven, the social worker who visited Mike's home.

"So, it was quite interesting, to say the least," he says with a rather rueful smile.

"How so?"

"Well, both parents were there and started off by insisting that nothing was really wrong. That Mike was just having a bad day when the neighbors saw him on the hood of his mother's car."

"I've sat on the hood of my mother's car." Doesn't sound too exciting to me.

"Oh, but have you thrown yourself onto the hood of your mother's car, grabbing the windshield wipers and screaming at her that she's not allowed to leave, while she's backing out of the driveway?"

"Oh my!" Mrs. Callahan looks startled. I can't blame her this time. Steven's words paint quite the mental image.

"Oh, it gets better. First they tell me that he's done that before but that it's no big deal because he always gets off when she stops the car and comes back into the house."

"She gives in to him?" Yikes. I start to judge, but then my mind flips back to this afternoon and my decision not to talk to Mike about Donny...just because it was easier than letting him escalate.

"Oh, yeah. Then we go on a tour of the house. They show me his room, which contains every toy and gadget you've ever seen, most of them broken and thrown around the place.

Then they show me his little sister's room, which has a lock on the door about an inch from the ceiling."

"They lock her in her room?" Will she be in my class next? Might be nice to have a girl.

"I'll get to that. Then we see their room. Pretty normal-looking master-suite deal. Until they close the door and show me how it's covered in gouges—big jagged slash marks all over the wood. They tell me—all calm and cool—that those are just the marks from when Mike has one of his tempers. It wasn't like they were showing it to me to demonstrate how bad things are either. It was just part of the tour."

"His...tempers?" Mrs. Callahan is growing pale.

"Yeah. His tempers. When he grabs a kitchen knife and chases them into their bedroom. When they go in and shut the door, he stabs it with a knife until he calms down."

"Oh my God! And his sister?"

"Well, usually she's in the master with them. Only some-times, when he's in a 'mood' and they have things to do, they lock her in her room, just in case." He shakes his head, and I shudder a little at the thought of a young girl locked in her room so that her brother can't—

And that's as far as I can take it.

"So what happens now?" I'm not sure I want to know.

"I don't really have a clear answer. It's a strange case. There's no evidence of abuse here. He is clean, clothed, and healthy. His sister has never been hurt. The parents haven't either, as far as I know. It's a volatile situation and will be put under investigation, but there's no quick or easy answer. Chances are, there will be a recommendation for family counseling and maybe parenting courses."

"That's it?" I'm incredulous, but at the same time I can't think of anything better off the top of my head, which is exploding with all of this new information about an already scary kid.

"I don't know for sure. That's what's most likely anyway. He sounds like he needs intensive help—even residential. But the spots are few and far between. He hasn't really done . . . enough…to snag one."

"So he actually has to stab someone first?"

"I don't want to answer that. Suffice it to say, it sucks for everyone. I have told his parents they should call 9-1-1 next time he goes off, or try to get him to the emergency room, but I don't think they'll do either one. It's a mental health issue, like with most of your students. Too many issues, not enough solutions. The local mental health clinic is our best— our only—bet right now."

"It's all so crazy. If you'll pardon the word." I'm shaking my head like a bobble-head doll.

"It's the right one. I'm sorry to tell you all this and then not be any help with it. Once they get into counseling, the clinic will work with the school. We can even set up some sessions here."

"When will it start?" Mrs. Callahan asks briskly, looking at her calendar as if getting everything organized into little squares will fix the unfixable.

"When there's a spot. I'll try to fast-forward it as much as I can, but everything comes with a waiting list. Anyway, I'll leave you my card, and you can contact me if there are any more concerns." He hands us each a card, shakes my hand, and leaves.

I stare at the card as if it might have some answers. Someone has to answer for all of this. Someone has to tell me why these kids have to completely bottom out before the system can find a way to help them claw their way back to the surface again.

✗

I tuck the card away in my pocket, along with the rest of the day. I have to put it all away before I pick up my girls from the daycare. I can't bring any of this home with me. I can't let the insanity of the world my students have to live in bleed over into the relative stability I'm trying to create for my daughters. I have to check the teacher at the front door and walk in as a mother.

"So, she did it again."

"Uh-oh. What *it* was it this time?" My three-year-old is high-spirited and fiercely self-protective. Which is code for the fact that she bites.

"Same old. She bit Jenny. Who bit her back. I was tempted to put them in a room and just let them have at it. Get it out of their systems."

The head teacher of the pre-K room, Sue, grins at me. I respect daycare staff as much as I do social workers. I used to be one, and I know how hard it is to work with large groups of tiny children, many of whom have overprotective parents with guilt complexes. Daycare teachers spend all day with our youngest, most vulnerable and valuable citizens. Most of us can barely cope with one three-year-old. Imagine a whole room full of them.

"You know, there used to be a theory that the best

medicine for biting is to bite back." I look down at my little blonde cherub. She looks like an angel. Looks can be deceiving. Just ask her sister. I know I should say something strong and parent-like to her about the need to keep her teeth to herself. But it's been a long day, and I just want a hug.

"Yeah, well don't try that theory. I don't want to have to call Children's Services on you. You seem like a good mom after all." Sue pats me on the head. I swat her away laughing. We used to work together a lifetime ago, before I switched over from tiny orange time-out chairs to large, ugly time-out rooms.

We go down to the "big kids" room to pick up daughter number two, who, at almost eight, no longer bites anyone, as far as I know. Gives one hope.

Driving home I think about Sue's comment. I know she was kidding around, but I wonder if she meant it. Do people see me as a good mom? I imagine the parents of the children my daughter bit today don't think so. Is it my fault that she bites? Is she acting out over the separation? Did she bite before we separated? I can't remember.

My instant gut reaction to hearing about Mike's home situation was to blame his parents. It must be their fault that he's so terribly out of control that they have to lock their own daughter in her room. They must be weak and horrible parents to let him stab their bedroom door over and over again without having figured out that he needs serious help.

My daughter chews on other kids. I tell her no and laugh about it with her teacher and then let it go, figuring she'll outgrow it. Is that how it starts? Was Mike a normal little kid who bit people when he was frustrated and then just didn't grow out of it? Is it his parents' fault? Or did he arrive with something inside of him already broken?

Am I responsible for everything my children do? And will do in the future? Am I to blame when they do something "wrong"? Do I take the credit when they do something well? Is my mother responsible for everything I am?

I don't know where I end and they begin.

I don't know where they end and I begin.

CHAPTER 12

Bombshells and volcanoes

"So, good news! The board has officially designated your class a class."

"What?"

"Your class. It's been given full status, which means I—we—get additional funding. It's an integration-based behavior class." Mrs. Callahan is practically rubbing her hands together with glee. I wonder if she's planning to redecorate her office.

"So, does that mean I can get some of my own workbooks?" At the moment, I beg, borrow, and most often steal supplies for my kids from other rooms. I also spend a fair bit of my salary on resources from the local teacher store, trying to find ways to interest the boys in learning. I am supposed to be paying attention to their academics...somewhere between social skills, life skills, and keeping them from killing each other.

"Well, we'll have to wait until I get the numbers, and then we'll figure it all out. In the meantime, they've set the cap at ten full-time, twelve with part-time integration."

"What?" I say it again. My ears work, but my comprehension is having trouble. Ten *what*?

"You're to have no more than ten full-time students with the option to go to twelve if we have students who can spend more than fifty percent of their day in the regular stream." She smiles brightly. She thinks this is some kind of an accomplishment. I just stare at her blankly until her smile falters.

"Anyway, I guess you need to get down to your room. We'll chat later."

Chat? We'll *chat* later? About the potential number of students in my room creeping up to ten or even twelve? Is she kidding me? We're struggling enough with the number we have, and she wants to double it?

As of two weeks ago, four became five with the addition of Chris, a complicated little guy who brings a whole new set of challenges to the room. He's only nine, with a head full of ringlets and piercing brown eyes that are as shrewd and calculating as Mike's blue ones, but with less apparent malice. Chris doesn't seem all that interested in beating up any of the others. He's mostly interested in running away.

He lives at home with his mother and father. There have been some incidents in the past that have made school staff suspect some level of abuse in the home. He has never arrived at school with bruises or anything like that. The problem is that he says things that demonstrate an unusual level of sexual understanding. There's a concern that he's been shown pornography or has been present when adults are engaging in sexual behavior. There's an even bigger concern that he's been molested. The very thought of it makes my heart clench every time I look at him. Chris is very bright and well-versed in the art of diverting questions about his home life, so no one has ever been able to confirm or deny these suspicions. Apparently he was found in a school bathroom one day, blocking the exit route of a little guy who still had his pants around his ankles. There was no proof that he did anything but scare the other child, but the incident resulted in the decision that he needed to be in a placement where he could be watched all the time. As in, he can't go to the bathroom without an escort.

How could we watch him that closely if we had ten or twelve kids coming and going?

Oh, right, the other thing we were told is that he was put on a waiting list for a psych assessment. The estimated wait time for his case is eighteen months. That's the equivalent of almost two full years of school. In the meantime, all we can do is follow him around.

Chris can read, write, and do arithmetic. He's smarter than I am and knows it. He's a lot more manipulative than we were expecting. Watching him is a full-time job.

Watching Cory is also a full-time job. And Donny. And Kevin. And Mike. Especially Mike.

Mike hates Chris with a vengeance. Mike needs to be the smartest one in the room. He needs to be controlling the show, under the radar when he can and right in our faces when he can't stay low enough to keep out of trouble. He's been in the time-out room more than all of the other boys put together. I keep telling myself that he's in there for de-escalation not punishment.

But it's hard to see the difference sometimes. Most of the time.

And Mrs. Callahan wants me to be excited because I now officially have a class, which might mean more money. And will definitely mean more kids. And doesn't seem to mean more staff.

She obviously has absolutely no concept of what we do in a day.

We're all going to lose our minds. And maybe a student or two.

✗

"The cabs are almost here." Sean's voice startles me out of my silent panic attack.

"Okay, coming," I answer, but he's already gone off down the hall. The cab drivers don't stick around to be sure we've arrived on the scene. We learned that the hard way, arriving a split second too late to prevent a full-on fistfight between Donny and Cory. We haven't been late since.

"You the teacher?" A voice calls out to me from inside the first cab as I arrive at the drop-off area. I walk over to the cab.

"Yes. Is everything all right?" I peer into the back. It's Mike. He looks angry. Not a good start.

"No. Kid here didn't want to come to school. His father managed to make him get into my car, and then he kicks my seat the whole way here, swearing at me like a trucker. Next time, tell his father I don't want him."

I take a moment to be impressed that Mike's father forced him to do something. Anything. Makes me wonder if the counseling sessions have started without anyone telling me.

"I'm sorry. We'll take care of it." Not sure why I'm apologizing. I didn't kick anything.

"Okay, kid. Out of the car. I have to go." The driver looks at Mike in his rearview mirror. Mike kicks the seat, square in the driver's back.

"Fuck you."

"Mike. Out of the car." Firm, authoritative. Hoping against hope that I don't have to pull him out kicking, screaming, and foaming. I see Sean out of the corner of my eye. He's got the other four guys by now. He's likely trying to decide if it's safe to leave me on my own.

"Sean, could you please take the boys to the room and call down to see if Ms. Jackson can come and help you get the day started? Then could you give Mrs. Callahan a call and ask her to come out here?" Sean nods and ushers the boys into the school.

"Mike. I would like you to get out of the car. Now. Mrs. Callahan is coming, and she won't be too happy that you're detaining this gentleman from his job." Although I don't imagine Mike is afraid of having his father called or being suspended or whatever other principal-style threats usually scare students somewhat straight.

I don't imagine Mike is afraid of anything.

"I don't give a fuck."

"Kid, out of the car!" I want to tell the cab driver to stay out of it, that he's just going to escalate the situation, but I don't. After all, it's his cab. He's the one who has to drive the kid here, all alone, every morning. It's a ridiculous situation when you think about it. I don't know what Mike's capable of, but I don't think there are too many limits.

The impasse seems to have gone on forever when Mrs. Callahan finally arrives.

"Is there a problem here?" She looks into the cab and then at me.

"Fuck the hell off!" Mike screams at her from the backseat.

"Oh," she says. She looks at the driver.

"I'm reporting this to my boss," he says as Mike kicks him in the back of his seat again.

"I see. Young man—"

"Mike." She looks at me briefly as I interrupt. Her eyes tell me to shut up.

"Mike. You have three seconds to vacate this vehicle. You are trespassing on this gentleman's private property, which is not going to be tolerated."

"What're you going to do about it, bitch?" Mrs. Callahan doesn't even flinch.

"If you are not standing calmly on the sidewalk by the time I count to three, the police will be called, and you will be removed forcibly by them. One...two..."

And the door opens and out he comes.

So I guess he is afraid of something. Maybe we can hire a cop to hang out in my classroom for the rest of the year.

"And there will be no more of this today. Understood?" She's glaring at him with hard, principal-quality eyes. I've never seen this side of her before. I have to admit to being a tad impressed.

Maybe now she'll understand what I'm dealing with, and there'll be no more talk of ten students.

Mike nods without looking at any of us. Mrs. Callahan looks at me.

"Well then. I guess everything's fine now. Have a nice day!" And she's gone back to the sanctity of her cozy little office space, leaving me to escort an extremely angry Mike to the classroom.

It's not even nine o'clock, and I'm pretty much ready to go home. Between Callahan's little bombshell and Mike's charming performance in the cab, this day is already pretty far away from being nice.

We walk into the classroom where the other boys are already sitting at their desks, looking about as thrilled as I feel. I have to do something to turn this day around, or it's just going to go from bad to worse.

We need to do something fun.

I stand at the front of the room, waiting for morning announcements, trying to think of something we can do that won't result in total chaos. If I was still teaching Resource, this is one of those days when I'd make the kids redo all of my bulletin boards.

I don't have any bulletin boards in this classroom. Nothing sticks to the painted brick walls except paint.

Except *paint*.

"Sean? Can you hold down the fort for thirty seconds? I just have to run down the hall to see if Mr. Z's in his room. Boys, I can still hear you when I'm out there!" I try to look menacing before I dash down the hall to our see if Mr. Zeeman, our beloved and multitalented custodian, is in his office. He's there, and I quickly explain what it is I want to try to do.

"Sounds fine to me. Just put some soap in the paint, and it should wash off fine," he says, smiling. I can tell from his eyes that he thinks I'm a bit nuts. That's okay, though. He's probably right about that.

I run back down to the classroom, praying that they're still behaving moderately well so that I don't have to cancel my idea.

"So, we're going to do something different today!" I blurt out somewhat breathlessly. My announcement is not greeted with excitement. Different is not always better in their worlds.

"We are going to paint a mural on our back wall! Spruce up this place a bit!" I smile encouragingly at Sean, who looks a little pale at the brilliance of my idea. I hurry over to the sink and start digging around in the cabinets underneath. There are still all kinds of art supplies under there from when this was a "regular" classroom, and I manage to find several cans of paint and a few brushes that still have pliable bristles.

"So, here you go. You can work together to come up with a theme, and you have the whole back wall as your canvas. Go for it!"

They all sit there looking at me with the same basic expression Mr. Zeeman had on his face. Everyone around here thinks I'm nuts.

"You want us to paint on the wall?" Donny asks, looking more than a little dubious.

"Yup. It's fine. Mr. Zeeman said it's okay. You can paint whatever you want. Well, almost anything." I smile encouragingly. Donny looks at Cory and shrugs.

"Cool. Let's go. Come on!" Chris hops up and heads over to the paint. No one wants the new guy to get first crack at the wall so suddenly everyone's on his feet, even Mike, who seems to be coming out of his funk. Sean and I try to stay close enough to keep some sort of order, but far enough back to let them come up with a plan on their own.

"Seriously, we can just, like, paint all over the wall?" Donny asks again, paintbrush poised ready to strike.

"Seriously."

And so they do. After a remarkably few seconds of intense consultation, all five of them grab brushes and start to paint. Sean and I watch in fascination, and a little trepidation, as masses of brown, black, orange, and red paint find their way onto the wall. At first it looks like the boys have decided to go the abstract art route, but after a few minutes a shape begins to emerge.

I start to laugh as a giant volcano takes its place on my classroom wall, complete with rivers of lava pouring out of the exploding crater at the top. A few dismembered bodies appear to be floating downstream, with what looks like blood dripping out of various orifices.

It doesn't take a psych degree to figure this out.

"Um, did you ask Mrs. Callahan about this?" Sean asks, staring at the wall as if unable to tear his eyes away.

"Not exactly," I answer, smiling widely as I imagine just how much she is going to enjoy the new decoration on my wall.

Now I'm having a nice day.

CHAPTER 13

In the middle of the night...

There is a moment in the deepest part of the night when the sky is so impossibly black that it seems to disappear from sight. Street lamps and stars compete with one another to light the way for travelers who dare to venture out into a world that only exists for an instant before time flies in to spirit it away.

It's a time of night, or perhaps more accurately morning, that I discovered when my girls were babies and eager to eat at 2:00 a.m. When I was pregnant I dreaded the infamous two o'clock feedings. A rampant insomniac for most of my life, I did not relish the idea of being awakened night after night by a squalling baby who would expect me to feed her and would then fall asleep while I stayed awake trying to remember the latest trick for falling asleep.

When it actually happened, I discovered a moment in time that I never really knew existed. So late that I felt no one else could possibly be awake. The world seemed to belong to me and my little girl, soft and dark and safe. My mind felt clear and relaxed; sleep came easily for the first time in my adult life.

I'm the only person I know who was disappointed the first time my newborn slept through the night.

Two o'clock has lost some of its magic now that worrying about life wakes me up instead of a hungry baby. The darkness isn't quite as soft and definitely not as safe as it fills up with worries that keep me awake.

I'm sure Callahan is sleeping soundly, peacefully planning the very ways in which we're going to spend all the exciting money that's going to come our way, courtesy of our new "class."

A class. A self-contained, special-education class, if we're going to be honest. At a time when the powers that be in the world of education have decided that such things are of the past. Of course, it's not the first time that decision has been made, and it won't be the last. The endlessly cyclical world of education tries on new philosophies the way most of us try on new shoes—squeezing our toes into sizes and shapes that don't necessarily fit, but which we wear anyway, because they look good.

Mainstreaming. Integration. Desegregation. It's called different things. It means that all children have the right to be educated in a "regular" classroom with their peers. And as a philosophy, I'm totally on board. If one of my girls had a "special need," I wouldn't want her shoved into a dark corner somewhere so that she's hidden away from the rest of the school.

But it isn't that simple. At least not to me. I've worked with children with all kinds of so-called special needs. Most of them can survive in a classroom setting so long as they have a teacher who has the proper resources, training, and student-teacher ratio—a fairly rare combination these days. But there are some kids who just don't seem to be able to survive in a regular classroom setting, at least not in our current system. They seem to need to be somewhere smaller, more intimate, where the world is more tuned in to their needs. Maybe just for a while. Maybe for a long time. It depends on the individual.

And that is really what education should be, shouldn't it? Individual. But if we're going to be brutally honest, we have to admit that it really isn't. For any child. Take a regular class, like my daughter's third-grade class. She was born in December. Her best friend was born in January. That means the two girls are almost a full year apart. A year is a lifetime to a seven-year-old. The amount of development that goes on between seven and eight is huge. But the system is set up so that those two girls are taught and assessed as if they were at the identical level of intellectual and emotional development. It's like making them wear the same size clothes just because they're born in the same year. Everyone's a size three, even if they're not.

Maybe the old one-room schoolhouses had it right after all. Put everyone together in one place, have the older kids help the younger ones, and teach everyone at the level that fits them best.

Of course, I'm good at complaining, especially inside my own head in the middle of the night, but I don't have any brilliant solutions. Not yet anyway. I don't know if we should have self-contained classrooms for some students or just smaller regular classes with more staff for all students so that there's more time to find out what everyone needs. I do know that adopting sweeping philosophies that push all children into a single ideological pile ends up leaving some of our most vulnerable children in the dust, while teachers end up feeling frustrated when they can't give their students what they need.

The phone starts ringing and knocks me off my internal soapbox with a resounding thump. Who could be calling me in the middle of the night? This can't be good.

I run down the hall, heart pounding in rhythm with my feet, praying that it's just some over-enthusiastic telemarketer from overseas who doesn't know about the time difference.

"Hello?" My voice is breathless from a combination of being out of shape and full of panic. At least I know it isn't about my girls. They're here, safe with me.

"This is Dermott Williams. Mike's father."

Mike's father? That's pretty close to the last person on earth I would have expected to be on the other end of the line. Unfortunately, I don't have to wonder how he got my number. The curse of living in a small town means that there are only two people with my last name in the phone book. This is not the first phone call from a parent. It is the first one at this hour though.

"Mr. Williams? Is everything okay?" *Stupid question. A parent is calling me at 2:00 a.m. Everything is most definitely not okay.*

"No. Mike won't calm down. He's out of control, and we don't know what to do!" Now I recognize sounds in the background. The guttural screaming that means that Mike has completely lost it. Lost himself.

"Mr. Williams, you need to call the police and maybe an ambulance as well."

"I don't want to do that. He's...just a boy. I thought maybe you had a...trick or something that you use at school...something I could try." His voice is heartbreaking as he pleads with me to use some kind of magic wand that will transform his raging monster of a son back into a child.

"No, there's nothing I can do for you. You have to call for help. He needs to see a doctor. A psychiatrist."

"He's not crazy! He just gets angry sometimes!" The noise in the background is escalating. I can hear a woman's voice pleading for peace.

"I didn't say he's crazy. I just mean to say that you need professional help—beyond the school or even the clinic. And you need it now."

"I don't know—"

"Please, Mr. Williams. He needs to get to a medical facility. For all of your sakes." My voice is shaking.

"Okay. I'll try to get him there." And he hangs up before I can say anything else. My hands are shaking now and my stomach feels sick. I don't know if I did the right thing. I don't know what I should have done. Or not done. I don't want to be responsible for this. I don't want to even know about it. It's two o'clock in the morning.

I get up and walk down the hall to my daughters' rooms. I need a reality check. My reality.

My girls are sleeping soundly, as usual. I stand at the door of each of their rooms in turn, watching them, wondering about their dreams. They look peaceful and innocent. I want to believe that they're dreaming about peaceful and innocent things.

Does Mike's mother sneak to the door of his room when he's sleeping? Does she look at his nine-year-old face and wonder where the terrifying angry young man comes from? Does she wonder about his dreams? Does she fear them?

She must feel so...helpless and horrified by her own son. How can you bear to watch every little piece of your child melt away like that until he's nothing but a puddle of rage splashing everyone in his path?

I wonder about my other students. Are they sleeping soundly? Do any of them have a mother who stands at the door watching them sleep?

Not Donny. At least, not anymore. Do foster moms watch their foster kids sleep?

I haven't met Cory's mom yet, but from a few brief conversations on the phone, I don't imagine she takes the time to stand and watch him sleeping. I try to imagine Cory sleeping. He's such a perpetual-motion machine that I can't see him staying still, even at two o'clock in the morning.

Kevin lives with both parents and a younger brother who is, as his mother told me proudly, "basically normal." Kevin's mom definitely loves him in her own somewhat obsessive-compulsive way. Obviously a family trait. It's quite possible that she watches him at 2:00 a.m., perhaps hoping he'll talk in his sleep and tell her things that he can't when he's awake.

I wonder if Baby sleeps with him. I wonder if she talks in her sleep.

I don't want to think about Chris's family and what goes on at his house at 2:00 a.m. I'm going to have enough nightmares filled with Mike and his parents to make the rest of the night rough enough.

Actually, I don't want to think about any of them for the rest of the night. It's just too sad. It makes my heart hurt.

It's almost 3:00 a.m. I need to go to sleep. Right now.

I need to not think about going to sleep, because thinking about it keeps me awake.

I need that magic wand that Mike's father seems to think I have so that I can use it to make myself fall asleep before it's time to get up. Tomorrow—I mean today—is going to be another tough one. If I show up missing any of my faculties, everyone will know. Even the whale.

Of course, if I did have a magic wand, I wouldn't have to go to school at all. I could just wave it over everyone, sprinkling happy fairy dust in their hair, making all of their troubles go away and putting myself out of a job.

Abracadabra, your life no longer sucks.

I really need to sleep.

CHAPTER 14

Splash pants and ladders

After a sleepless night, I arrive at school early so that I can fill Mrs. Callahan in on the phone call. She seems quite surprised and concerned about it and assures me that she'll look into the situation. She then advises me to put it out of my mind and just get on with my day.

Easy for her to say.

Forty minutes later, I'm standing with Sean waiting for the cabs to arrive, filling him in on the events of my night. As we stand there, me talking and Sean shaking his head in amazement, the first car pulls up and deposits none other than *Mike* on the sidewalk. I stare at him in something pretty close to shock. He looks at me with something pretty close to disgust, which is his usual expression. Actually, everything about him looks...usual.

Sean glances at me, eyebrows raised as if to say "are you sure you got that phone call?" I'm wondering the same thing. Did I dream it? I figured he'd be in the children's ward at the psych hospital this morning. Not here! How can he just be here? How can his parents have sent him to school without a single word to me about what happened after 2:00 a.m.?

The rest of the guys arrive, and Sean and I take them down to start our day. Cory is wound up as usual, and Donny had a bad night at the foster home, and Chris is acting a little jumpy, and Baby is taking flying lessons—basically a normal day, but busy enough that I don't have time to follow up on Mike right away. I have to rely on Mrs. Callahan for that, and I don't imagine I'll hear from her any time soon.

Mike looks pretty calm. That's not always a good thing with him. He epitomizes the phrase "calm before the storm." I really need to know what's going on.

"Ms. S? There's a call for you." The voice interrupts a math lesson that no one is really listening to.

"Oh, good. Is it Mr. Williams?"

"No, it's your daughter's teacher."

All thoughts of Mike evaporate as my heart literally leaps in my chest at the instant electric shock of mom-panic that zaps through me. Both my daughters' teachers know what I do here. Neither of them would call unless it's an emergency. I look at Sean.

"I'm okay for a minute. Go!"

I know I shouldn't leave him alone, but panic trumps reason, and I head down to the phone in Mr. Z's office, where I can still be close enough to hear my class if anyone erupts.

Not that I can hear anything but the pounding of my heart at the moment.

"Sharon—I'm out of my room for a moment," I call into the class across the hall, as if somehow telling the junior kindergarten teacher will cover me for leaving my class.

I grab the phone and press the blinking light with a shaking finger, ordering myself to calm down. I don't even know which daughter it is.

"Hello?"

"Oh, hi! It's Janet. Sorry to bother you."

"It's okay. Is everything all right?" My little one just started junior kindergarten two weeks ago. I wasn't planning on putting her into school this year, figuring one more change would be too much for her. But on her fourth birthday, she announced to my parents at her birthday supper that she was starting school the next day. I had been telling her for a while that school was for four-year-old girls not three-year-old girls, and she took me literally in the way that only a child can. No amount of persuading could sway her from her absolute conviction that she was supposed to be going to school.

So like the firm and authoritative parent that I always am, I gave in to a four-year-old on an issue as big as where she's going to spend her days. Well, her alternate days anyway. Monday, Wednesday, and alternate Fridays at school, and the rest of the time at daycare. Sounds disruptive to me, but so far she's been doing great. Until now that is.

"Oh, yes. She's all right. It's just that she won't put her splash pants on."

"What?" Once she said the words "all right," I let my attention drift a little, turning one ear toward my classroom. I don't think I heard her right.

"She's refusing to put her splash pants on. It's very damp and cool out today."

"You called me because she won't put her splash pants on?" I wonder if I sound as stunned as I feel.

"Well, I wasn't sure what you wanted me to do." She sounds like she thinks this is a reasonable call. My teeny tiny four-year-old won't put her splash pants on. That's her teacher's biggest challenge so far today?

That's not fair. I work across the hall from a JK room. I hear things. It's not easy. But seriously. Splash pants?

First biting. Now splash pants. My little behavior girl.

"She probably doesn't want her skirt to get wrinkled. Just tell her she can't go out without them. I doubt she'll want to stay in. Or better yet, send her out without them, and let her get her new leotards dirty. That'll be a life lesson for her."

"If that's what you want…" She sounds hesitant and somewhat disapproving. She'll probably go down to the staff room at lunchtime and tell all the other teachers what a bad parent I am.

"Yes. I have to go now." I barely get the words out when I hear a shout from the vicinity of my room and see a familiar body go flying past. I look down the hall to see Sean standing outside the classroom.

"Switch!" He calls, starting down toward me. I head his way.

"Mike said something to him. Not sure what. I'll follow him."

"He's heading out of the school. I'll have to call Mrs. C." I yell the last bit at him as he disappears out the door at the end of the hall.

I press the intercom button and ask for Mrs. Callahan. "It's Chris, Mrs. C. He's headed out the back door. I need Ms. Jackson to cover my class so I can help Sean retrieve him before he's off the property."

"I'll head outside and see what I can do until you get there," she says.

Great, Callahan to the rescue! I wasn't really asking her to do that. Sean and I are better on our own. Chris is still an unknown quantity to us, and we're really just trying to figure out what his triggers are, so we can avoid them. At the same time, he's trying to figure us out and is doing a much better job of it.

"Chris took off. Where'd he go? Why does he do that all the time? Runs away instead of smashing Mike's face in."

"Cory, that's enough. Just...do your work." Cory is squirming in his seat with the excitement of it all. The only thing better than being in the middle of a problem himself is watching someone else in trouble.

"Like to see you try smashing my face in," Mike mutters to his desk, just loudly enough for Cory to hear him.

"Mike. Never mind. We don't have time for this right now." My voice is weary instead of tough. He looks at me, considering whether to push it or not.

"Whatever."

I don't bother breathing a sigh of relief because it's probably not over. Donny hasn't weighed in yet.

"Hi. Mrs. Callahan said you need to go." Ms. Jackson has arrived. She's really a super hero. Comes down here whenever she's asked without any complaint or seeming concern. Bet she can leap tall buildings too.

"I do. Chris is having some trouble. I hope we won't be long. I expect you all to behave."

Chances are they will behave, but I probably should have put an adverb in there somewhere.

By the time I finally get outside, I can just barely see Sean and Mrs. Callahan standing on the far side of the yard. As I make my way across the pavement and onto the grass, I realize that they're standing in the backyard of one of the houses unfortunate enough to back onto our schoolyard. I hope the people who live here work during the day, otherwise the noise at recess would be deafening.

If they are here, I imagine they're wondering why there are two adults standing in their backyard looking up into a very tall tree.

"He's up there?" I ask needlessly. *What do I think they're doing—bird watching?*

"Yup. Skittered his way up there like a squirrel." Sean looks impressed.

"Chris. I think it's time to come down now!" I try to raise my voice enough to carry up to him while not sounding like I'm actually shouting. It's harder than it sounds.

"No! Mike's a jerk."

"Sometimes. You still need to come down and deal with it on the ground. I don't want you to get hurt."

"You don't care if I get hurt! You just don't want to get in trouble!"

"That's not true. We do care. I would like you to come down."

"Come on, bud. It's time to chill." Sean joins in.

"You don't even know me. You don't care about me. I

could fall out of here right now, and you would forget all about me by tomorrow."

"That's not true."

"Enough! I can't have him hurting himself. We have to get him down right now, or I'll have to call the police." Mrs. Callahan joins the conversation, using her no-nonsense voice.

Again with the police. Is this going to be her new refrain? We can't control the little criminals ourselves, so we're going to call the cops? Then again, that's exactly what I told Mr. Williams to do last night. This morning. Whatever.

"Just give us a few more minutes."

"No. It's time for him to come down." I am expecting her to run back into the school and call 9-1-1. What I am not expecting her to do is grab the bottom branch of the tree and start pulling herself up the side of the trunk, high heels, silk skirt, and all.

"Mrs. Callahan, I don't think climbing up after him is a good idea!" I look at Sean in a panic. What is she doing? She thinks she can...what...climb up there and carry him down over her left shoulder like some panty-hose-clad firefighter? Sean shrugs and grins a little.

"I don't see anyone doing anything more constructive," she grunts, scrambling awkwardly up to the next branch. One of her shoes falls off, almost impaling me in the process. I bet she did that on purpose.

"Mrs. Callahan—" I don't know what else to say. I'm sure as hell not going up after her. This is a really, really bad idea on every possible level.

Sean's grin widens as shoe number two tumbles down, and Mrs. Callahan keeps on climbing in her panty-hosed feet. She's surprisingly agile for someone her age. Actually, I don't know how old she is, but I assume she's a lot older than I am. And I don't think I'd be able to get up there.

"Phew. I'm just about there!" she calls down as she reaches the branch just below where Chris is sitting, silently watching her progress and shaking his head.

"Ms. S! I think I'll come down now!" Chris yells, ignoring Mrs. Callahan completely. He nimbly and quickly climbs down the tree. Sean's right. He does have an impressively squirrely quality to him.

"Ready to go in, bud?" Sean asks cheerfully, putting his arm around Chris's shoulder in a friendly half hug that I can see is tight enough to hold him in case he runs again.

"Yeah. But Mike better keep his mouth shut!"

"Agreed." And off they walk, two buddies just sauntering across the yard without a care in the world.

I look up. Mrs. Callahan is clinging somewhat precariously to a branch about twenty feet off the ground.

Maybe it's the lack of sleep, but I really, really, really want to laugh.

"Are you okay?" I ask loudly, trying to mask the borderline hysteria that is about to break loose.

"I am fine. However, I would appreciate it if you would contact the custodian and inform him that I am in need of a ladder," she answers, sounding as dignified as a principal up a tree could possibly sound.

"Will do!" I turn quickly, literally running back to the school. I almost make it to the door before the laughter overcomes me. I laugh and laugh until I start to cry.

Mr. Zeeman looks a little startled when I appear at his

door with teary eyes and flushed cheeks. He looks even more startled when I inform him that he needs to take a ladder next door to get his boss out of a tree.

There are moments when I really love my job.

CHAPTER 15

Field tripping

"You want to do what?" Mrs. Callahan looks at me with an exaggerated expression of astonishment.

"I want to buy some kind of pet for the class. Teach them a little compassion and responsibility." I turn my lips up in what I hope looks like a reasonable smile.

"There are allergy restrictions. Not to mention the reality that anything living in your class will likely end up dead."

I open my mouth to give her the response that she deserves. But calling her a dickhead probably won't get me my way here, so I suck it up. I even try a little chuckle, as if I agree with her.

"I'm talking about something like a hamster. In a cage. Something they have to feed and clean up after. Something they can care about."

"I don't know. These are pretty rough kids."

"Things have been going a bit more smoothly recently. Chris hasn't run anywhere in a few weeks. Donny seems more settled. Kevin is actually working once in a while. Cory... well, he isn't beating people up every day."

"And Mike?"

"He hasn't had any real issues since the phone call. At least not here."

She nods slowly, and I imagine that we are both flashing back to the conversation we had after she finally managed to get down out of the tree and return to her office, with both her dignity and her pantyhose in shreds.

"I finally spoke with Mr. Williams," she had told me, "He did go to the hospital after phoning you. They kept Mike there three hours for observation and then let him go."

"That's it? No follow up? Nothing?"

"From what Mr. Williams told me, they didn't feel they had reason to keep him once he calmed down."

"So, he just comes to school?"

"Well, he didn't have any real issues today, did he?"

"No more than usual, but that isn't the point. He could have. The kid was up all night!"

"I'll talk to Daniel Norton about the situation and see if he can find out whether the counseling has started yet. I didn't think to ask Mr. Williams. Did you?"

"Not at 2:00 a.m., no." I remember Mrs. Callahan had smiled at me, almost kindly, I think.

Turns out that the incident did jump start his counseling. A very small lining of silver in an otherwise pretty dark cloud. Maybe the clinic can figure out how to help the whole family.

Back to the present. Mrs. Callahan is watching me with impatient eyes. I guess I'm the only one flashing back. She's sitting comfortably in the here and now waiting for me to talk.

"I guess I think we need something that will make us feel more like a regular class...instead of just a bunch of people sharing space. You know?"

Callahan looks at me with an expression that clearly states that she does not know what I'm talking about at all.

"I think it will take more than a hamster to make your class regular." She makes it sound like we all could use some laxative.

What we could use are some resources. Maybe daily psychological support. A time machine, so the kids can go backward and find a better start to their short lives and a chance for a better finish.

"I know. But we have to start somewhere, and I really think this might be a positive thing for them—us. Oh, and I want to take them with me to choose the pet. A field trip." I say it quickly so she doesn't have a chance to say no before I can get it out into the air.

"A FIELD TRIP?" I can hear the capitals.

"Yes. Like other classes do. Only smaller. Sean and I can handle it. We'll just go to McDonald's and then the pet store and back here. Two hours. Tops."

"I don't know. The liability issues—"

"The permission form covers all of that. The boys have been with me long enough that I trust them to do this. How will they ever have a chance in the real world if we keep them out of it?" I try to look earnest and honest as I lie through my teeth.

I don't actually trust them at all. How can I? I have no idea what they're like outside the walls of this school. That's not true. I do have some ideas, none of them particularly good ones. I know that a field trip could be an unmitigated disaster. But I want to try. I want them to believe in themselves a bit. Or at least think that I believe they can do something "normal." I want them to share something besides our classroom and a rather impressive vocabulary of profanity.

She looks at me for a moment. I can see the word *NO* forming on her lips. She closes her eyes for a second and shakes her head. "All right. Make sure the forms are signed at least a week before by the proper guardians. If it all falls apart, it's on you."

"Okay. Good. Thanks." I'm so shocked she said yes that I can't make sentences.

For the next three weeks we engage in "how to go out in public properly" lessons. It's amazing how much we take for granted in this area of kids' development. I'm not talking about manners—the *pleases* and *thank yous* and *excuse mes* that don't really mean very much to anyone. It's the little, real-life things, like knowing how to start a conversation, or how to ask for help appropriately, or the best way to react to criticism, constructive or otherwise, without punching someone in the head. There's an assumption that children are just being rude when they don't demonstrate the social niceties that we've decided are signs of a civilized person. But some kids, like my guys, actually don't know much more about social skills than they do about algebra. They need to be taught about social variables and how to manipulate them properly with the same care and attention that we shower on math skills. In our classroom, social-skills lessons take precedence and are taught in all kinds of ways, from very specific step-by-step instructions, to reading social stories and books, right through to role playing, the class favorite. The kids particularly enjoy the performance-art variety during which Sean and I act out potential problems and they have to come up with solutions for us.

We've had a few strange looks from people passing by the room as I yell hysterically at Sean while he gives me a lecture about finishing my homework and the boys roll on the floor laughing. Those lessons sometimes get away from us, and I'm not sure how much learning goes on. Although having fun is a social skill too, and learning how to come back from a silly situation without losing control is one we're all still working on.

Finally the big day arrives, and we head out to find our new classmate. We have a real school bus, smaller than most but still yellow and still different from what the kids are used to. The bus is actually tiny, one of those charmingly referred to as a handicapped bus, as if it isn't as strong or capable as all of the other buses. Even though there are lots of seats, Donny and Cory manage to have a fight over who gets to sit with Kevin as they walk up the steps of the bus.

"Hey, guys! No one fights on the bus. There are two trips anyway, so you can share. Now sit down and zip it or you aren't coming!" The bus driver, an obvious veteran in the world of yellow buses, is glaring at the boys, who both stop in their tracks. I can tell they're wondering if they should get into it with this new person who thinks she can boss them around. I really hope they don't. I want this trip to work, if only to prove Mrs. Callahan wrong.

Cory takes his fighting stance, feet planted, hands fisting. I put my foot on the bottom step so I can fly up and intervene, but Donny beats me to it, reaching over and touching Cory on the arm. He shakes his head and walks past him, sitting down behind Kevin. Cory shrugs his shoulders and follows, plopping himself beside Kevin.

The rest of the trip is charged with excited energy, and Sean and I have a few more close calls with overstoked emotions before we finally arrive. We even make it into the restaurant and manage to get food ordered without anyone getting a black eye or any other such drama. If you don't call the one little fistfight in the lineup dramatic, that is.

"Okay guys, garbage in the can, coats on, and we're gone. Cory, Donny, please don't start that again. The pet store is expecting us." I'm not supposed to say please when they're threatening to beat each other's brains out for the umpteenth time. Authority figures do not assert their authority by using mannerly words. It sounds too much like begging. But I've been overly well-bred and can't seem to stop.

The pet store is directly beside the restaurant, and the boys troop in with remarkably little fuss. The pet store owner is kind and matter of fact with them. He doesn't appear to see anything strange about us, and the boys seem to respond positively to his attitude.

"So, what do you think?" With the exception of Mike, they're all peering into a cage with a pile of little rodent bodies scuttling around. Mike is standing back, hands in his pockets, looking very bored, like he considers himself far too cool for field trips.

"I like that one," Donny says, pointing to one of the bodies, which looks the same as all the other bodies.

"Does everyone agree?" The other boys either nod or shrug. Donny has become an unofficial class leader over the last little while. I don't know if that's because he's the oldest and the tallest or if it's some other quality that I can't really define as yet. But the other boys seem to give him a modicum of respect—which is far more than they give to anyone else most of the time.

Except for Mike. Mike mostly ignores him when he isn't trying to trigger him.

"Excellent choice. I'll package him up for you." The storeowner seems enormously pleased. Donny smiles a little self-consciously. It makes my eyes water a bit, and I feel a little sniffle coming on.

"Come on, guys, help me take Fred to the bus." Sean picks up the cardboard box containing our new class mascot. Fred. I have no idea why the hamster's name is Fred other than it being the end result of a rather loud and long lesson on the concept of democratic voting.

I stay at the cash for a few moments to pay while Sean herds the boys into something resembling a line, and they march out to the bus, a ragged army of misplaced soldiers heading back to the front.

Our brave bus driver smiles as the kids pile on, patiently watching them as they insist on pushing through the door two or three at a time instead of heeding my request that they try the single-file method. I think I accidentally said please again. The kids could each have their own seat, but they insist on sitting together, which would be a sign of positive social growth if they didn't use the close quarters as an opportunity to push, shove, hit, and curse each other out. I sit at the front, body turned sideways and legs out in the forbidden aisle, and Sean sits at the back, hamster securely held in his lap so that he at least makes it home alive. I have his shiny new cage and bags of shavings and food sitting beside me in a large, environmentally un-cool bag.

After the first few minutes, the kids start to calm down, lulled by carbohydrates into a state almost approaching peaceful. I just start to congratulate myself on the wonderfulness of my plan, on my wisdom and understanding of the needs of my students, and on standing up to my principal when the bus driver's voice interrupts me.

"Oh my God!"

She's screaming the words, and at first I can't understand why because none of the students are anywhere near her. I spin around to look at her, and she's pointing out the front window, frozen in a tiny fraction of a minute that's broken off from the universal timeline to complicate our lives. My eyes follow the direction of her shaking finger, and I suppress my own scream. A half-ton truck is coming toward us down an icy hill, spinning in endless three-sixties. I stare at it, the spinning hypnotizing me so that I don't immediately recognize the danger of what's about to happen.

The bus driver unfreezes and grabs the wheel with both hands, twisting to the right as hard as she can to avoid the unavoidable. I glance out the window and see the yawning abyss of a deep ditch, kept away from us by a tiny cable fence that wouldn't hold up to a mountain bike. The kids are noticing now, starting to make loud sounds, and I know I should turn around and figure out some empty lies to comfort them, but I can't tear my eyes away from the pseudo fence that is going to make the difference between life and death.

The truck finishes its mad arabesques with a deafening crash as it pounds into the bus. Unsatisfied with its performance, it flies over us in one final leap before crashing to the ground to await our ovation.

CHAPTER 16

Blood and vomit

The bus finally stops moving, and I feel myself joining in the dance, doing my own flying leap out of my seat and onto the floor. I can hear crying and shouting all around me. My glasses are gone, and I feel around on the floor for them.

"Ms. S! Ms. S! What happened? What happened?" The voices are in my ear, and I should stop crawling around on the floor and figure out if the kids are all right, but I need my glasses. I can't do this without my glasses.

"Ms. S! Ms. S! Ms. S! Ms. S!" Each "S" is louder than the last, but my hands still scramble madly across the floor until my fingers finally stumble on a familiar shape. I grab my dirt-smeared and probably totally scratched-up glasses, cram them on my face, and take a deep breath before I force myself to look around. I don't really want to. I don't want to know that they're hurt. I don't do blood and pain. I'm a teacher, not a nurse. The two worst things that can happen in my classroom are vomit or blood. When I see vomit, I always feel the need to puke my own guts out in sympathy. When I see blood, my head goes light and fuzzy, and I feel like I'm going to faint.

"Sean?" I call his name first, needing to know that there's another adult here to help with the blood and vomit.

"I'm okay. I think."

"Ms. S, Ms. S, Ms. S, Ms. S!"

"It's okay everyone! We're all right. Sean and I are going to check you all out carefully. Just sit tight." I push myself to my feet, checking to see if I have all my body parts before seeing if the students have theirs. The first one I find is Donny, pushed down on the floor beside his seat, wedged tightly, head on his knees.

"Donny, honey? Are you okay?" Stupid question but the only one I can think of. *Are you okay with the fact that I took you on a stupid field trip to buy an even stupider rodent and almost got you killed in a bus accident?*

"I don't know," he answers weakly, raising his head to look at me with tear-filled eyes. I feel the bile rise up in my throat as my brain starts to fill with bubbles of horror. His face and chest are covered with dark, viscous slime, and I can't see where it's leaking from. He's crying harder now, eyes and ears both pouring out fluids that mix with the slime, making a volcanic mess that I know I should be trying to clean away. I dig through my pockets and find a small napkin, which I use to dab ineffectually at his face.

"What hurts?" I know in some forgotten part of my

previously intelligent mind that he might not even know, that shock might be numbing his nerve endings.

"Nothing. I don't want you to be mad, okay?" He looks up at me with his teary-eyed, snotty, slime-coated face.

"Mad? Why would I be mad? You didn't cause the accident." I've heard of this. What's it called? Some kind of guilt thing.

"No, not that. My sundae. You told me to throw it out, and I didn't, and now it's all over the place. All over me." He reaches his hand into his jacket and pulls out an almost-empty ice cream sundae cup. Chocolate sundae. Not blood on his face. Hot fudge. Dark, goopy, slimy left-over hot fudge. Psycho blood.

I start to laugh, which turns into tears without my permission. I stand up and pull him to his feet, looking around to see where everyone else has ended up. Sean is moving between the seats, limping a little but otherwise seeming to be intact. He already has Kevin and Cory beside him. Kevin is looking out the window and shaking his fist.

"Fucking truck! You fucking truck! Fuck off you fucking truck!" He's saying it over and over and over again. I'm so amazed to hear him talking without the whale that I don't say anything about his choice of words. Besides, I totally agree with him.

"I was upside down on the seat. Upside down. I, like, flew across the seats and fucking landed upside down!" Cory is jumping up and down and pointing to a random seat. "Want me to show you?"

Before I have a chance to say no, he flings himself at the seat and lands on his stomach with his feet kicking around in the air behind him. He's laughing, but I'm afraid the pressure of the seat on his full gut will make both of us puke, so I make him get up.

The other two boys are still sitting down, looking pretty stunned but not particularly upset. I take a deep breath, which starts out to be one of relief.

"Off the bus! Everyone off the bus now! She's going to blow!" The bus driver's screams slam into me, making me choke on my relief. I look up toward the front of the bus where she's standing, pointing out the back window. I follow the direction of her hand and wish I hadn't. The truck has burst into flames.

"Quickly. Get the kids out the front before we catch!" She stands there, captain of the sinking ship, ushering the children past her and out onto the snowy shoulder of the road. She refuses to leave until Sean and I are also safely out.

"Run!" She shouts at us as she scrambles down the steps. We look back, wondering if we should be helping the truck driver, but Good Samaritan cars have now stopped, and we leave the rescuing to them. Without taking the time to line them up, we just start herding the kids down the side of the road. Suddenly, Mike stops.

"Fred! Fred! He's going to blow up! You have to save him!"

Fred, the source of all this excitement, is still sitting in his box on Sean's seat at the back of the bus.

"I'll get him," Sean says, reversing direction and heading back.

"No, it's not safe!" The bus driver yells at him, but he ignores her. I know I should tell him not to go. To come back and save himself and let the hamster die.

But Mike wants him saved.

Mike expressed a real concern for something other than himself.

How could we stand there and let the hamster die? The whole point of this field trip was to find something for my kids to care for. Everyone told me it was crazy to think that a class full of emotionally messed up behavior kids could possibly take care of a pet. They told me it was even crazier to actually take my kids outside of the relative safety of the school and into a world where there might be real people who might see us. That they would embarrass me at the pet store and probably kill someone at the restaurant.

They were perfect gentlemen at the pet store, and there was only the one fistfight at the restaurant.

And now Mike wants us to save the hamster! Letting it die would absolutely be the wrong thing to do.

It occurred to me much later on that standing there and letting Sean die would probably have been a bad thing also.

Thankfully, Sean did not die. He bravely entered the not-yet raging inferno, emerging mere seconds later with the box in one hand and the giant bag in the other.

"Let me see him!" Mike demands loudly. Sean looks at me quizzically. We should really be running down the road, but from experience we both know that arguing with Mike would take a lot longer than just giving in. Giving in is even weaker than saying please, but there's a time and place for everything.

"Ok, quickly." The boys crowd around as Sean carefully lifts a flap of the box. I can't resist a peek myself and finally finish my breath of relief when the little guy looks up at us, then scurries around the bottom of the box without a care in the world.

"Now run, but keep together," I yell, and we all take off down the side of the road with Kevin's refrain keeping us in lockstep.

"Fucking truck, fucking truck, fucking truck, fucking truck, fucking truck."

Chris is at the front of the pack, using his considerable running experience to pace us. I'm really hoping he doesn't just keep on going until he finds whatever it is that he's looking for.

Within seconds we come to a white farmhouse straight out of a Norman Rockwell painting. Perfectly maintained barns line up a short distance behind it, likely housing perfectly maintained cows, judging from the smell.

"Chris! Hold up now," I'm panting along in the middle of the pack. I am seriously out of shape. There's no way I could catch him if he decides to keep going.

"Okay!" he calls back and stops. I take a second to catch a couple of breaths. This is *so not* the way I envisioned this field trip.

Field trip? Is the fact that we very nearly ended up dying in a snow-covered field irony—or just insanity?

"Okay, guys. We're going to go to the door and ask these kind people if we can please wait inside their house until we can figure out another way back to the school. Remember, we are asking for help from strangers, so we need to be polite." Social-skills lessons at ten below zero, thirty seconds after a truck tried to kill us. Teacher of the year.

I walk up the driveway and onto the wraparound porch that probably has pots of daisies on it in the summer. I imagine a woman inside, comfortably middle-aged in a flower print dress with an apron on that says something like "home is where the heart is." She'll take one look at us and take pity, then invite us in for tea and crumpets.

The kids straggle along behind me and stop. I look at them for a moment and shake my head. She'll more likely scream and head for the root cellar.

"Remember, inside voices and keep it polite. Actually, try not to talk at all." I ring the sunflower-shaped bell and try to smooth my hair and my nerves a bit while waiting for someone to come.

"Hello?" The door opens to reveal a woman a few years older than me. She's dressed in a power business suit and has a phone glued to her ear.

"Oh, hi. Sorry to bother you, but we've had a bit of trouble and need your help." I'm pretty sure she doesn't have any crumpets. At least she doesn't scream and run away.

"Bruce? There's someone at my door. I'll have to call you back. What happened?" She speaks quickly, and it takes me a second to realize she's turned her attention from her phone conversation to our live one.

"Fucking truck hit our bus," Kevin says helpfully.

Donny pats Kevin on the back and smiles like a proud papa. She looks a little startled, but laughs a bit. I shrug my shoulders and nod.

"Could we just stand in your front hall until I can get someone to pick us up?"

"Oh, of course. Poor kids. I thought I heard a crash, but I wasn't sure. Come in."

"Remember guys. Polite. Kevin, I'm super happy you're

talking, but maybe no more talk about trucks, all right?" The kids push past me and stand uncomfortably in the hallway, a motley and pathetic little crew. I suspect I don't look any better than they do, a suspicion confirmed by our benefactor's eyes when she looks me up and down in that way certain women have.

"Are you a teacher?" She says the word with the slightest emphasis, making it sound vaguely embarrassing.

"She's our teacher. Ms. S." Donny steps forward, and she steps back. He wipes his hand across his face, smearing the sundae mess even further. She takes another step back.

"Are you all okay?" she asks from a safe distance.

"Fucking truck hit our bus," Kevin says again, as if that explains it all. Which I guess it does.

"Kevin, what did I say about talking about the truck?" I say it gently, putting my hand on his shoulder. He looks at me and nods. He stands there for a second sniffing, and I wonder if he's starting to cry. I've never seen Kevin cry, but today would be as good a day as any to start. First talking. Now crying. He's turning into a real live boy.

He sniffs again, and I squeeze his shoulder a bit. He looks up at me and sniffs one more time. Poor little guy. Poor all of us.

He looks away from me and over at the woman who was kind enough to invite us into her home. She smiles at him encouragingly, and I feel a little swelling of pride as he steps a little closer to her, looking up at her with big serious green eyes. Is this it? The moment when he shows me he's actually picked up a social skill or two from all of my endless lessons?

"Smells like shit," he says.

CHAPTER 17

Aftermath

We arrive back at the school on a second bus they sent to retrieve us. There's little fanfare heralding our return. Mrs. Callahan greets us at the door with what looks like something less than overwhelming concern. I suspect from the look in her eyes that she was feeling more satisfaction than anxiety over the outcome of my experiment. Not that I think she's happy we had an accident. Just that she was right. I bet she's reveling in an I-told-you-so moment, although my perception might be somewhat off. I'm pretty sure I'm in some level of shock.

"You need to go to the hospital immediately. I'll arrange coverage for your class," she says firmly.

"I'm fine," I lie. I'm not really fine. I feel like a truck hit me.

"Go anyway." Even more firmly. I suspect that this is not a sudden outpouring of concern for my health and welfare. This might be more of a concern over what the teachers' union will do if I'm not taken care of properly.

"I'll go after they leave. If I go now, they'll all freak out. You don't really want to deal with that, do you?"

She looks at me for a moment. She's wrestling with herself, her face twisting into different expressions that she's totally unaware of. I can see the battle between her fear of my students and her fear of my union. It's a short battle.

"Fine. There's less than an hour before their cabs come, I guess. But make sure you go as soon as they're all gone."

It occurs to me after she leaves that she didn't say anything about taking the children to the hospital. I don't even think she's going to call the parents and guardians. I know that no one seems to be hurt, but I would certainly expect to be called immediately if something like this had happened to either of my children.

Then again, I'm not sure that everyone here thinks of my guys as children at all. They're just behavior kids. Screwed up, violent, rude, and socially unacceptable. Tough as the proverbial nails. Nothing can break them.

Not even an out-of-control half-ton truck.

Maybe my students need a union. Kevin can be their rep, now that he's talking.

The rest of the afternoon is preternaturally quiet. Shock can do that.

"It's so quiet in here. Maybe you should have more accidents." The head pops around the corner, disembodied and dis-empathetic. It belongs to Ms. Keller, our vice-principal-slash-sixth-grade English teacher. I've seldom seen her anywhere near my classroom. She doesn't appear to notice that the children are still here.

"Fuck you, bitch," says Kevin. Speaking for the group—including me. I can't help but swell with pride. He's still talking!

"Are you going to let him get away with that?" the disembodied head is asking me.

"I didn't hear anything. Guess my ears are ringing from the accident. Good thing because that way I can say I didn't hear you either. And then I won't have to do anything about the fact that you came into my class and interrupted me with my students just to say something ignorant."

The accident has loosened my tongue…unhinged my inhibitions. Maybe I should go to the office next.

"Well!" The head sputters incoherently and withdraws. Presumably to float down to the staff room to share with the other talking heads.

"Awesome, Ms. S." Cory high-fives me. My shoulder hurts when I raise my arm, but I'm too brave to let on.

"Owww!" Well, maybe not *that* brave.

"You okay, Ms. S?" Donny looks at me, concern producing wrinkles on his eleven-year-old forehead.

"Yeah. I'm all right."

"Ms. K's such a bitch," Chris pipes up from where he's lying on the floor. I'm not sure why he's down there, but at least he's still here, so I haven't said anything about it.

"Probably better if you find another way to say that." Social-skills lesson number seven hundred and ten.

"Ms. K's a total and complete fucking asshole of a bitch."

Chris smiles up at me. I shake my head at him, trying to look disapproving. A smile creeps across my face instead.

"Hey, Kev. You really told that truck off!" Donny's sitting on a chair beside Kevin's desk, helping him pretend to do a word search puzzle.

"Fucking truck hit our bus."

"Totally." Donny nods and scribbles over another word that isn't really a word.

"Hey, he likes his cage!" Cory is at the back of the room helping Sean get Fred settled. Everyone but Mike goes back to check it out. His concern for Fred's health and happiness seems to have been left behind on a snowy road somewhere in farm country.

"You all right, Mike?" He's sitting quietly at his desk, staring at a book that I'm pretty sure he isn't reading.

"Yeah. Why wouldn't I be?" He looks at me with his usual look of total disgust.

"No reason." *Maybe you get attacked by trucks every day, but it's new to me.*

Half an hour later, the boys head home and I head to the hospital. I shouldn't be heading anywhere. I should be on the phone calling parents and guardians, but Mrs. Callahan wouldn't let me stay. She told me to go and not to worry about it. That she would take care of everything.

I really hope that's true.

Three thirty in the afternoon, and there are only four people in the waiting room. Looks like a short wait.

A few minutes later, the triage nurse disabuses me of that assumption. "Actually, the doctor is not here yet, so you will have a bit of a wait. We have a few people in the examination rooms already, so you'll just have to sit tight." She smiles at me cheerfully. I smile back, somewhat less cheerfully. Small town hospitals. Fewer people in the waiting room. Fewer doctors in the examination rooms.

Still better than the city, though.

I don't even know why I'm here. Nothing really hurts. My back feels a bit sore, but nothing's bleeding, and all my body parts are still attached. I'd rather just pick the girls up early, order a pizza, and have a Care Bears movie marathon.

Sean isn't here. I wonder if he's one of the people already in the examination rooms. Once we got back to the school, he admitted that he had a pretty deep gash on his leg that looked stitch worthy.

I sit down carefully. Guess my back is more than a bit sore. I wonder how the kids are doing. Will the ones who have parents at home be going to the doctor tonight just to be sure they're okay? Will Donny get checked out too? Will anyone make sure they aren't traumatized by the disastrous end to our very first field trip?

What the hell was I thinking? That's what everyone will ask. Everyone thought I was nuts to try to take them anywhere. Bunch of messed-up behavior kids shouldn't be allowed out in public, after all. I'm sure the fact that the accident had absolutely nothing to do with my kids won't occur to anyone.

My kids.

My class.

I hate to admit it, but sitting there together in the aftermath of our accident, it occurred to me—for just a moment—that we felt like a unit for the first time. A group that belongs together instead of some random collection of individuals that all want to be somewhere else.

Just for a moment.

But maybe it was a start. Maybe I should tell Callahan that my experiment worked after all.

Except that we didn't need a hamster.

All we really needed was a random act of vehicular violence.

CHAPTER 18

Glow bugs and raccoons

This is where it would be nice to say that the accident was the turning point in our year, the climactic peak in the storyline of our lives that would lead to a dénouement of happily-ever-after for everyone.

It wasn't exactly that, but it did seem to be the start of some subtle changes to the group dynamic. No, that's wrong. It seemed to be the start *of* a group dynamic, period. Other than random moments, like painting volcanoes or laughing at bad acting, my class has always been mostly an every-kid-for-himself environment. But after the field trip, every once in a while we actually started to feel like…well, a class.

One of the most interesting aftereffects of the accident was Kevin's suddenly loosened tongue. We knew he *could* talk—obviously it wasn't the whale who had been conversing with us all this time—it's just that sometimes we forgot. So when he started talking himself, it felt like something of a miracle.

Of course, talking is only step one. Trying to expand his vocabulary to something approaching socially acceptable is becoming a bit of a class project. His grammar and syntax seem to work just fine when stringing together profanity. And although Baby has always been a pretty good talker, every-day conversations seem to be a challenge for Kevin when he's appearing as himself. Everyone but our lone wolf Mike is pitching in to help Kevin figure out how to use his own rather deep and gravelly voice as effectively as he uses his sweetly high-pitched Baby voice.

"Bathroom," he growls at me one day. Donny looks over at me with a bit of a conspiratorial grin. He whispers in Kevin's ear.

"Go to the bathroom," he growls a bit louder.

"*May I* go to the bathroom?" I say it slowly and clearly, modeling it for everyone. Kevin looks at Donny with a puzzled look on his face and then back at me.

"Sure, go ahead," he says, pointing in the direction of the door, his words drowned out by the howls of laughter from Donny, Cory, and Chris. I think I even heard Mike chuckle, but I can't be sure.

Kevin's newfound skills in language are a welcome addition to his report card. It gives me something to say. Our school board insists that I use the same form as everyone else, the one that focuses on reading, writing, math and science, and all of those other subjects that get short shrift in my room. There's one tiny section at the end for social-skills development that I'm supposed to use to sum up six hours a day of nonstop social-skills intervention and programming.

And this is only step one in the fun that comes with the midyear reporting period. Step two is trying to explain the so-called reports to the parents and guardians when they come on parent-teacher interview day.

If they come.

"Oh, I don't think I'll be able to come in. Marjorie either. We don't really see the need. We've talked to you a few times, and he seems to be doing all right." Mike's father is polite.

In actual fact, the last time I spoke with him was on my home phone at 2:00 a.m. I don't think that really counts.

"Well, Mr. Williams, I really do have a number of concerns that we need to discuss. And I would like some idea of how things are going at home, now that Mike is in counseling."

"Oh, well, that. Well, that's not a concern now."

"Pardon?"

"I mean, he isn't going. None of us are. He was being… non-cooperating. Um, I think they said hostile. So we're done for now."

"I really think you and your wife need to come in to talk to me about this and about Mike's progress in general." I'm trying to hold on to a professional tone, but my sheer astonishment is making it hard. He's done? How many sessions could he have had? I've never even had contact with his counselor, and now he's *done*?

"Well, maybe another time. Have to go now."

I stare at the phone as if it might have an answer or two for me. No one else does. He's not in counseling? Because he's too hostile? I thought that was the reason for counseling in the first place. How can he be out of it for the same reason he's supposed to be in it? And how can his parents choose not to come and talk to me?

And who's going to answer all of my questions?

Strike one.

Strike two is Donny's foster mom. Even though he's been there a while now, his placement is technically considered temporary, which is kind of interesting when you think of it, because I thought that foster placements were pretty much all considered temporary. Anyway, his foster mom doesn't really have the time to attend an interview for him when she has so many scheduled for her other kids. His social worker is busy this week. His mother isn't supposed to come to the school until all of the issues concerning the assault charge and custody are resolved one way or the other, which doesn't seem to be happening any time soon.

I wanted to speak to the social worker and the foster mom. I have concerns. All Donny talks about is going home to be with his mother permanently. Every day it comes up in some fashion. He makes her cards and writes her letters continually. It's pretty close to an obsession, although I'm not sure that's the right word to use for someone who wants something that he's actually supposed to have.

Anyway, I want to know what's going on. Is he really going home? What am I supposed to say to him when he talks about her? Or when he says he's going home for good?

Mostly I just say nothing. And feel useless while I worry about what all of this uncertainty is doing to his already confused and volatile outlook on life.

So, interview day will be short and sweet: Chris's and Cory's mothers and Kevin's parents, which is fine, because I have to get over to my daughters' school and attend a couple of interviews of my own.

Attending a parent-teacher interview when you are both things yourself is strange, especially when you work in the same tiny town where your daughters attend school. There's an awkwardness to the conversation, a stilted formality as you sit down with someone who is essentially your colleague to talk about your own child. It can be particularly uncomfortable if the news isn't good.

My daughter's grade three teacher is an old friend with whom I worked at my first school. She's pretty happy with overall progress, but has some concerns about inverted writing and spelling—mirror image, to be exact. In other words, my daughter can write entire sentences backwards, every letter and every word, so that you have to use a mirror to read it.

"She's just creeping up on her eighth birthday. It's still pretty natural for some kids at this age. Especially seeing as she's a December baby, which makes her younger than most of the other kids. I'll keep an eye on it." I'm trying to sound like a mother, but I know I'm coming across as a spec. ed. teacher know-it-all. I see it in her eyes.

"Well, we'll keep an eye on it here. I'll let you know if we want to consider going ahead with testing." That's code for *You don't know everything, especially when it comes to your own kid.*

"Thanks. And I will let you know if I think she needs it." That's code for *I do so!*

We smile politely, both relieved it's over, and I head down

the hall to the JK room. I haven't had any splash-pants-related phone calls recently, so I'm hopeful that things will go well here.

"So, I'll get right to the point," she says. This is not a good start. Points are sharp and usually painful.

"O…kay." I draw out the syllables.

"We're a bit concerned about her…fantasy life, I guess you'd call it."

Fantasy life? She's four. What other kind of life does she have?

"I'm not sure what you mean."

"Well, she's been telling some quite outlandish stories at sharing time. And it appears she believes them. We can't get her to admit that she's making them up."

"What do you mean?" *Outlandish?* What year is it, 1965?

"Well, she likes to tell the class about adventures she pretends to have had. With a girlfriend who she says visits her at night and takes her away to another land. Chloe?"

"Oh! Chloe. She's not a girl exactly. More of a bug—a glow bug." I smile cheerfully as I provide this all-important clarification. Her eyes tell me that she doesn't care. Or maybe they're just saying that she doesn't like glow bugs. I can't tell.

"It doesn't really matter. What matters is that she is convinced that this…glow bug?. . . comes into her room and takes her away to some place and brings her back in the morning. She tells us she's too tired to work sometimes because she's been up all night."

I laugh, but stop quickly at the look on her face. Oh. She doesn't find this funny. "Yes, she tells me the same stories. One time she even had her party shoes laid out beside the bed because she had been to Chloe's birthday party the night before. She has a very creative imagination." I grin proudly. It was so cute—little shiny-white party shoes so carefully set out beside the bed so that she could bring me into her dream world. I'm pretty sure it's a sign of genius.

"I understand that. And an imagination is a wonderful thing. But she doesn't seem to understand that she's imagining this Chloe and all the things they do together. She thinks it's real. I keep trying to explain the difference to her, but she won't listen."

She is obviously not buying the genius theory. "Oh, I see. Well, did you tell her Santa Claus and the Easter bunny are all in her mind too? Because last time I looked, they weren't exactly real."

"Of course not. That's not the same thing at all."

So it's okay to lie to kids about chocolate-loving bunnies and an imaginary fat man who only gives presents to rich kids, but my kid can't fly around at night with a glow bug?

"So, what is the concern here?" I ask in the politest tone I can dredge up, which isn't really all that polite because I am feeling more and more pissed off by the second. She looks at me like she thinks I'm really, really stupid. I just smile, even as I feel my fingers curling into annoyed fists.

"She will not admit that she is making up her adventures. I am concerned that perhaps the strain of your…situation…might be taking a toll on her. Have you considered counseling?"

"For her or me?" I hear there's a spot opened up down at the clinic.

"Of course it's up to you. I just wanted you to know of my concerns."

"Well, I appreciate it. And no, she doesn't need counseling. She's four. And I don't tell her that her adventures aren't real. They're real to her. I'm fine with that." I try to ignore visions of a stuffed black whale laughing in my face. *Back off, Baby.*

"Well, so long as you are okay with it. I just wanted you to know." *Great. Now she's offended.* It's really not a good idea to offend your child's teacher.

"I do appreciate your concern, and I will keep an eye on her. Are there any other problems? She's wearing all her outside clothes and keeping her teeth to herself?"

"Yes. Of course. And her academics are fine."

Gee, that's a relief. I'd hate to see her super important four-year-old "academics" slide.

And that was a snippy little thought. I think it's time to go back to school and sit on the teacher side of the desk before I say something out loud that I'm going to regret. Besides, I'm pretty sure my palms are starting to bleed where my fingernails are digging in.

✗

"So, you mentioned on his report card that he's finally decided to speak to you?" Kevin's mother looks very pleased. Good start for my team.

"He did. The day of the accident, actually."

"Oh really? And what did he say?"

What did he say? Something involving a four-letter word and a truck. Don't think I want to tell her that.

"I can't remember exactly. But we've been working on social language skills ever since. Asking questions. Having conversations. That sort of thing. The other boys are helping. Kevin still doesn't speak as well as Baby, but we're working on it."

"That's good. At home, Baby only comes out when we have company. It would be nice if Kevin could speak directly to our friends. Funny that the accident is making such a difference. We took him to see it, you know."

"See what?"

"The bus. We called the police and asked where it was. Kevin needed to see it for some reason. So we went."

"Oh, goodness. He never said anything." Of course he didn't. He still can barely ask to go to the bathroom.

"I just about passed out myself. I couldn't believe the damage. The bus is basically scrap metal now."

I shake my head. I don't think I want to see it. I don't want to think about how close my girls came to being half orphans.

"Well, I'm just glad everyone is all right."

"Anyway, I won't keep you. Just wanted to thank you for keeping him. This is the longest he's been in one school in a while. There's been so much moving around trying to find the right place. Now we just have to find the right diagnosis and we're off to the races."

"Well, if there's anything I can do—"

"I'll let you know."

She heads off down the hall, followed by her ever-silent husband, and I sit back to wait for interview number two. Or four, depending on how you look at it.

I don't think Kevin should even be in our class. His issues are so different from the other boys. He seems like he's on the autism spectrum more than anything, but I'm no expert. And the experts haven't managed to diagnose him with anything yet, so I've got him. Which isn't such a bad thing for us, seeing as Kevin still seems to be the classroom neutral zone. He doesn't bother any of the other kids, and none of them bother him—at least not in front of me.

"Excuse me?" A very small voice comes at me from the door of my classroom. An equally small woman is standing there. She's wearing large sunglasses that cover most of her face and a baseball cap over long, curly brown hair. She looks acutely uncomfortable and seems hesitant to come all the way into the room.

"Hi. You must be Chris's mom. Come on in!" In my effort to make her feel at home, I accidentally shout at her, making her cringe and shrink into herself. If I don't calm down, she'll disappear completely. I walk toward her slowly, the way you do with a skittish horse that might turn tail if you get too close.

"Would you like to sit down?" I try again, this time with a softer voice that's aiming for soothing. She nods slightly and perches on the edge of the chair.

"I know the report card isn't very illuminating. Chris hasn't been here as long as the other boys, so I really couldn't fill it in the way I would have liked."

"That's okay," she says in a whispery voice. She reaches up and pushes the ridiculously large sunglasses more firmly onto her nose. As they move on her face, I get a quick glance at the skin underneath her left eye. It's an angry shade of purple. I feel myself wince and hope she didn't see it.

"Chris is a really interesting young man. Very intelligent and capable. We just have to figure out a way to get him to channel his smarts into school work." I smile as if I've said something useful instead of filling the air with empty teacher talk. She smiles back very slightly and waits for me to say something else. But what?

I can't figure out how to talk naturally to her. She's so scared that I want to give her a hug. I want to ask her why her eye is purple and tell her I can get her some help. I want to ask her if Chris knows that someone hit her. I want her to tell me what happens to him at home.

I can't ask her any of those questions. I have to talk about school. Looking at her sitting there, I imagine that school is not the most important thing on her mind.

"So, Chris is working on all grade-level assignments right now. We feel he is a good candidate for integration and will be looking at that in the new year." I still sound like a robot. A teacher-bot.

"Integration?"

"A return to the regular classroom. We would start slowly and then gradually increase his time until he's ready to go back full-time." She looks at me from behind her glasses. I can't really see her eyes, but from her posture I suspect that they aren't filled with happy pride.

"I thought he would stay here with you." Her voice confirms my suspicion. She sounds panicked.

"Of course he will have my support as long as he needs it. Don't worry. We won't rush anything." I can't tell if my words pacify her at all. I shouldn't have brought the integration idea up so soon. I thought it might make her feel positive or something. I don't know. I seem to be making a mess of this interview.

"It's just…he had troubles at the other school. Saying things he shouldn't say. Does he do that here? Talk about… *it?*" I imagine that behind those glasses her eyes are begging me to tell her that he has stopped talking about things that he shouldn't even know about yet.

"There have been a couple of incidents, but we're working on it with him. That and running away from things instead of staying here and working it through are the two biggest issues that we'll be focusing on with him before any thought of moving him into another room." I feel like we're talking in code, both of us too polite to mention sex. Social skills.

"Okay. Thank you for helping him. I have to go. My baby girl will be awake soon." She gets up and scuttles from the room without looking at me. Her baby girl? There's a baby in the middle of whatever nightmare is being played out at that house?

This is crazy. There's obviously something very, very wrong in that household, and no one can do anything about it unless someone has the courage to admit it. We haven't had as many incidents of sexualized talk as there were at his previous school, but I suspect that's because it's more diffi-cult for him to get away from big-eared staff here. Most of the incidents at his last school involved his sharing detailed information with younger children, which then got reported to understandably horrified parents. We watch him closely all of the time here, especially with the JK room right across the hall. But stalking him isn't helping him deal with whatever is happening in his life.

Chris is too smart for us to get him to "disclose," and his mother is too scared. I suspect the father is the creator of the nightmare in the first place, although I've never met him. That only leaves the baby girl, who is not going to be saying anything any time soon.

There has to be another way in.

"Hi! Sorry I'm late! I'm Bobby's mom. I had a bit of a morning before I got here, but I'm here now, so let's get down to it!" A woman about ten years older than I am interrupts my thought when she sits down across from me, plunking a large cardboard box on her lap. Strange noises are emanating from it—scratching and a kind of gurgly squeaking sound. She opens up the top flaps and looks inside.

"Oh, it's okay, sweetie. We won't be long. I just have to talk to Bobby's teacher and we'll be on our way. Do you want to see him?" She looks up at me. I'm still wondering who Bobby is.

"Who?"

"This is Alvin. Like the chipmunk? Only he's not a chipmunk, are you, sweetums?" She reaches into the box and pulls out a raccoon. It's not a very big raccoon, but it's a live raccoon and not a very happy one. Sweetums has a large, red, oozing, festering wound on the top of its head. I press back against my chair.

"Oh, don't you worry. He won't bite you." She makes kissy noises in the general direction of the ooze. I try not to gag.

"I'll take your word on that. So, we're here to talk about Cory," I say, trying a gentle emphasis on his name. I am assuming Bobby is either Cory's brother or another wounded wild animal of some kind. Either way *I'm* here to talk about Cory.

"Cory? Oh right, of course. Cory." She shakes her head,

which makes the raccoon stir restlessly on her lap. I'm pretty sure there are laws against having wild animals in the school, especially the kind that ooze and live in a cardboard box instead of a cage.

"Yes, Cory. I know the reports aren't very helpful in telling you how he's really doing. I am hoping to change that for the second term."

She looks at me blankly. "Reports? I don't remember seeing any reports."

"Well, that's fine. They don't really say much anyway. Cory is showing some small improvements in his behavior. He is still very wound up much of the time, and it is relatively easy for any of the other boys to set him off, so we're working on trying to get him to slow down and think a bit before striking out."

"He does love to fight, doesn't he? His father was like that. Always using his fists. I do tell Cory not to be so rough, but he doesn't really listen, does he, sweetie?" I'm pretty sure it's the raccoon she's calling sweetie, not me.

"There are days that we get the feeling he hasn't had his meds at home, but he never seems sure when we ask him. Do you know anything about this?" On the days when we think he might be med-free, he's like the Tasmanian devil from the old Bugs Bunny cartoons.

"Oh, no. I'm not always there when he's getting ready for school. That damn cab comes so early, and I work late most nights. So he's pretty much getting it together on his own."

That explains the lack of meds and lack of lunch and the dirty clothes—the overall uncared-for vibe we get from him most days.

"Well, perhaps we can figure something out. Could you speak with his doctor about the meds issue? Perhaps there's a way that all of his daytime doses could happen here?"

"Oh, sure. I can just send the bottle in."

"Actually, I would need very clear directions, in writing, from your doctor if we're changing anything."

"Oh, well, I'll try then. Could take a while though. I'm pretty busy with work and this little guy. I found him in our backyard, all beat up. Poor little thing. I'm good with animals, you know. Bobby is too. He just loves them. Maybe you should get him an animal to look after here."

I glance toward the back of the room where Fred is making all kinds of noise on his little metal wheel. If I ever meet this mysterious Bobby, I'll be sure to introduce them.

"Well, thanks for coming in. We'll just keep working away here, and hopefully, I'll have a better reporting system for you by the end of term." She gives me an empty smile that matches my empty words. She gives Alvin one last snuggle and puts him back into his box, and they head off into the sunset together.

I wonder where Cory is today and whether he's had anything to eat yet.

I'd bet money that the raccoon had a hearty breakfast.

CHAPTER 19

In the wind

"Leave me alone!"

Donny is screaming. He's having a bad couple of days, compliments of the fact that he no longer lives in the same foster home. He apparently "lost it" a few days ago, verbally attacking his foster mom and then going on a rampage, a small tornado of pain ripping through the house, leaving considerable property damage in his wake. He was removed from the home in the middle of the night and plopped into another one before he even realized what he had done.

I do understand why his foster mother felt she couldn't cope with him. I admire the fact that she took him on in the first place. I don't know if I could do it. Take in a child who is so filled with anger and pain that it might spill over onto my family. Or worse, take in a child that I might fall in love with, only to have him returned home or sent away somewhere else. I can't imagine it. I can't even walk into an animal shelter without wanting to take them all home forever.

But at the same time, the system seems so cruel once a child ends up trapped in it. The inalienable right of childhood should be the understanding that home is home and that the people there love you unconditionally—that no matter how big the temper tantrum, you'll still be loved. Most of us couldn't stretch our imaginations far enough to understand what it would feel like to so suddenly and irrevocably lose your home. And in many cases, to believe that it's your own fault that you had to move on.

I know how hard Donny can be to deal with in the six hours we have him here in school, and I can only imagine how much more difficult, and dangerous, his behaviors could be in a home setting for the other eighteen hours of every single day. I know it's an almost impossible situation for everyone involved.

But he's still just a child.

They're all just children.

Children who are very close to attacking each other right at this moment in time.

"Donny. I need you to calm down. Tell me what's wrong." My voice is just loud enough to penetrate, and he looks over at me.

"Mike won't fucking shut up. He keeps telling me that I'm going to jail because no one wants me in their house and that my mother isn't ever taking me back, which is a big stupid lie!"

"Mike. I want you to leave Donny alone."

"Did you hear me say anything to him?" Mike's voice is its usual quiet monotone. Actually it's very quiet. Sean looks over at me as he slowly moves to our side of the room. We both know that the quieter Mike gets, the more likely it is that he's about to explode. It doesn't happen often, but when it does...

"No, I didn't hear you say anything. But I don't think Donny would make that up." I'm really wading into it here. Either of them is fully capable of lying just to have an excuse for what we not-so-affectionately call a "blow." Sometimes they're so desperate to get rid of all the poison inside them that they'll create elaborate fabrications so they have an excuse to explode. My eyes stray to the volcano that still fills our back wall.

"But you do think I would make shit up. You always take his side. It's like he's your little baby or something. Your favorite." He adds sarcasm to the last word, drawing it out in a soft but deadly voice.

"I don't have favorites. I'm a teacher. I treat you all equally." I honestly think Donny is the one telling the truth here, but I'm not positive. It doesn't matter, though—I shouldn't be engaging in this argument. I'm doing exactly the wrong thing. Something about this kid always puts me on the defensive, and I forget what little I know about dealing with confrontation.

"Bull...shit." And before I even register what he's doing, he's on his feet and his desk is flying across the room. It smashes into Donny's desk, sending him backwards.

"Fuck you!" Donny screams and launches himself at Mike. Sean steps between them, but it's too late. Mike has snaked around him and intercepted Donny's attack, and within seconds the two are on the floor, doing their best to murder each other. Before Sean can separate them, Cory comes out of nowhere and joins the attack. It's impossible to tell what side he's on. Mostly he seems to be somewhere in the middle.

"Cory! Leave it alone!" I have to join in the melee and try to pull at least one writhing body from the mess. I finally took that crisis intervention course two weekends ago, but it doesn't make me feel any better about this. I am afraid I'll hurt them or get hurt myself. I'm afraid they'll know I'm afraid, and that will make things worse. I'm afraid...of everything in this moment.

I manage to pull Cory off of Mike. He starts kicking out at me instead, and I struggle to remember how to get behind him so I don't get bruised. I have to get him into a safe hold so I can slow him down. It's so much easier to do this with a compliant adult in a training session. I wish I were working at the psych hospital where they have two fully trained people in every room so that teachers can just teach most of the time.

"Cory. You have to stop. This isn't your fight." He's not listening. Cory thinks every fight is his fight. He doesn't seem to differentiate at all between things that are happening to him and things that have nothing to do with him. He's always in the middle of everything, a lost soul trying to find somewhere to be, even if it's someone else's fistfight.

"He's beating on Donny. He's an asshole." He's writhing and trying to head-butt me. I'm dodging his head like an aging prizefighter who's lost his game.

"Sean will handle it. See? He's got Mike away from him

now." Cory slows down to look. It's true. Sean has managed to extricate Mike and is holding him tightly. Mike is revving up to full foaming mode, and Sean is trying to move him as quickly as possible out of the room and down to time out, where he can attempt to de-escalate Mike before anyone is hurt.

I need to get to the intercom to let the office know we're having problems, but I can't let go of Cory, and I can't take my eyes off of Donny, who is curled up on the floor crying. I feel like doing the same.

"Okay, okay. I'm done. Let me go!" Cory has stopped moving.

"I need to know that you are not going to go after Sean and Mike. That it is really done."

"Yes! It's really done!"

"Your voice isn't telling me that. I need to hear that you're calm."

"Okay. I'm okay." I hold on for another few seconds. It's almost impossible to know when it's safe to let go. It's almost impossible to know when it's safe to hold on.

I finally let go, and he sits down at his desk. He doesn't even look at Donny.

I close my eyes for a second to regroup and then look around the room. Donny is still curled up on the floor. Cory is talking to Kevin, who seems oblivious to the whole incident. And Chris...is not here!

"Where is Chris?" I don't know who I'm asking.

"Left," growls Kevin.

"Left? When did he leave? Where did he go?" My voice is loud and panicky.

Kevin just looks at me. Too many questions.

I can't leave the room to look for him. Sean is down the hall with Mike. I have no choice but to call the office.

"Can you let Mrs. Callahan or Ms. Keller know that I need some assistance down here. Immediately please."

"Will do."

"Like, right *now* kind of immediately."

"Got it. I'll get her down there now."

It only takes Callahan ten minutes to make the thirty-second walk from her office to my room.

"Chris is gone. I'm afraid he's left the building." I don't even give her time to ask.

"It's a little precipitous to assume that," she says. "We haven't even looked for him in the building."

"Chris is a runner. He always leaves the building."

"Where is Sean? Can't he go look?"

"He's down in time out with Mike. I don't even know what's happening there, and I should be checking. But I can't be everywhere. I need someone to find Chris. He's gone!"

She's not getting it. Chris is gone. He's a champion runner, and he could be anywhere by now. I don't even know how long he's been out of my room.

"I'll have Mr. Zeeman and Ms. Keller do a search of the school and the grounds, as well as the nearest backyards to the schoolyard. I imagine he's just hiding somewhere. Maybe he's back up in that tree."

And she leaves. Just like that. And I'm trapped here. I can't do anything. The other boys are staring at me, and I realize that I'm making my panic too obvious. I need to get myself under control so they don't lose theirs.

"Okay, guys. Let's get some math done." I smile brightly, as if math is the most interesting thing in the world. I take a few minutes to get them started on some hands-on math activities. Then I buzz the intercom again.

"Could you please ask Ms. Jackson if she could free herself up to come down here? I need to assist Sean for a moment."

I can't just sit here pretending to teach math. I have to find Chris.

My superhero arrives within a few minutes. I explain as much as I can of the situation and run down the hall to the time-out room. I peek in the window. Sean is sitting with Mike who seems to have calmed down. He still looks angry, but at least there's no blood or foam in evidence. Sean feels me looking and glances up. He gives me a thumbs-up, and I gesture for him to come over to the door.

"Chris has rabbited. Callahan thinks he's in the school, but I don't. She sent Zeeman and Keller to look, but I'm going to check the grounds quickly and the nearest backyards myself. I have a bad feeling that he's just gone."

I run outside, doing my best track time around the school, calling his name. I run over to the row of houses and scan the treetops. Nothing. I run back into Callahan's office.

"He's gone!" I puff the words in her face. "You need to call the police."

"We haven't finished a complete building search. We need to do that first. Just calm down and go back to your class."

"You aren't understanding this. He has a history of running away. There's something going on in his house. He could have been waiting for his chance to go. He could be anywhere! If you don't want to call the police, I'll do it. I'll take full responsibility."

"I have people searching the building and the grounds. I will make a decision about the police when that is done. You are not to call them. I will take care of it." She looks at me sternly. *What is going on now? She was pretty quick on the dial with Mike. Or at least she made him think she was ready to get police assistance. Now that we have a real crisis, she's Miss Independent?*

I head back down the hall, alternating between fury and panic. I go down to the time-out room to fill Sean in.

"What are you going to do?"

"I'm going to have to go over her head this time. It'll piss her off, but she's just wrong here."

I make my way to the phone and call the board office, looking for Daniel. He's not available, so I quickly explain the situation to the office admin there. She's familiar with my program and knows the kind of kids I'm trying to deal with here.

"I'll talk to the superintendent and get the okay for you to contact the police. I'll call you right back."

As I'm standing there waiting, an announcement comes across the general intercom, asking me to come to the office. I head down quickly, hoping that maybe I was wrong. Maybe they have Chris there and he was in the school the whole time.

I arrive to find Mrs. Callahan on her feet, looking very annoyed. There is no Chris. "The Mallorytown police just called the director. The director!" I assume she means the Director of Education, our CEO, as he likes to call himself.

"About?" I ask, although I suspect I know.

"Your...student...is sitting at the Mallorytown police station." She drips a lot of disdain onto the word student. *My* student, not ours.

"Is he all right?" She looks at me as if I've missed the point.

"Yes. Apparently he hitchhiked from here to there. Fifteen miles. Two different cars picked him up, if you can imagine. The second one was smart enough to take him directly to the police, who then called the board office and informed them that they had one of our students."

"Should I go and get him?"

"We will both go. The police chief wants to speak with us about safety protocols. As does the director."

"Sounds like a good idea." I ignore the look she gives me and follow her out to the car.

We arrive at the police station after a silent ride. Chris is sitting in a chair, as docile as I've ever seen him. He smiles at me slightly. I give him a stern look. Mrs. Callahan goes over to him as if to start lecturing, but she's interrupted.

"I'd like to speak with you before you take him, please." The police chief ushers us into his office.

"This boy managed to get all the way here. I checked with local police. No one called them at any point to report him missing. I can't understand how this could be?" He makes it a question, looking from Mrs. Callahan to me and back again. She puts on her professional face and sits a little straighter.

"I apologize on behalf of my school staff. The program is relatively young, and we haven't put all the necessary protocols in place. I have instructed my staff that in future the police are to be called immediately if there is any suspicion that a child could be missing. Better to err on the side of caution." She smiles, carefully avoiding my gaze. I'm so astonished that all I can do is stare. I can't find a single word.

She's trying to hang this on me. Making me look like the bad guy. She's got skills; I have to give her that. She should be in my class. She'd fit right in.

Next she'll try to hang me out to dry with the director, too. But she doesn't know that I called the board office and ratted her out already. This is not going to go her way at all.

She's going to be in trouble. The thought sings its way inside my head and gives me my first smile of the day.

CHAPTER 20

The red-eyed reindeer

I never did get the satisfaction of knowing how much trouble Mrs. Callahan was in for ignoring me the day Chris disappeared. She kept it to herself. The good news, though, was that the incident made the director notice my program and decide that filling it with students before actually giving me any real resources might not be such a good idea after all. He told Mrs. Callahan that she wasn't to accept any new students without his permission and that she had to figure out a new classroom for me for next year, one that's closer to the office so that I have more access to assistance.

This is all sounding wonderful—except for the seeming assumption by one and all that I am still going to be doing this next year.

This was supposed to be temporary. *Temporary insanity.*

Anyway, next year is a long time from now, and there's still lots to be done this year. I feel like Sean and I can breathe a bit more easily knowing that Callahan isn't going to drop kick any more kids into the room—at least not without some proper notice and maybe even some information about the next lost soul to find his way to us.

I say "his way" automatically, inside my head and out. There don't seem to be any girls heading my way any time soon. It's not that girls don't have serious problems. There were several girls at the Section school. I think the problems are there, but the presentation can be different much of the time, at least in the school setting. Girls often seem quieter and less overtly physical, able to fade into the background while their male counterparts kick and scream their way onto teachers' radars. I have a friend who works at a group home for girls, and it's her opinion that girls are even harder to work with than boys because they often try to hide their issues, and whether they're hurting themselves or others, it's frequently done in a way that's not immediately obvious to staff. All kinds of damage can happen before anyone realizes that something is going on.

My boys tend to end up with me because they're behavior is loud, proud, and out of control in a very observable fashion. Most of the time anyway. Which is why I am totally astonished when Arthur, our shop teacher, comes to me with a proposal.

"I have some gaps in my schedule for the next couple of weeks, what with students preparing for the Winter Holiday concert," he begins, "and I was wondering if you would like to try a project with your boys in the shop."

"Really? In your shop?" I must look as astonished as I feel because Arthur laughs.

"I know the tools all look big and scary, but there aren't many kids, and there are three of us. I can pull in a volunteer or two to ensure one-to-one support. We'll use the bigger, bolted-down equipment. It'll be good for them to do something hands-on."

I agree fully. So long as none of them decides to cut someone's hands *off*.

"Great. But I guess I'll have to run it past Callahan... Mrs. Callahan."

"No problem. I already did so. She seemed most pleased."

"Seriously?" I bet if *I* had asked, she would have reminded me about the bus fiasco and laughed politely in my face.

"Yes. Anyway, I have a nice project—each of the boys can make a wooden reindeer decoration. It's a simple pattern that can be cut out with a jigsaw and then sanded and painted by hand. I'll do a lesson on all of the tools just for interest and then a safety lesson as well. I figure about three visits to the shop and then the sanding can be done in class."

"Sounds great!" I say it too loudly, as if trying to convince both of us of the greatness of the plan. I do think it's wonderful, awesome even, that Arthur is taking an interest. I've actually noticed several teachers starting to pay some positive attention to my students since the accident.

I wonder if taking my guys into the woodworking shop as a first foray into the "regular" school setting seems a tad extreme. It's a pretty scary place.

"Super cool. They'll love it!" Sean's enthusiasm is unblemished by any concerns at all.

"You don't think we'll lose an arm or a leg in there?"

"No. It'll be like the pet store. They'll be so amazed that someone is letting them do something normal that they'll be cool. My group home kids are like that when we take them out on weekends—most of the time anyway." He smiles brightly to gloss over the last few words. I return the smile and shake my head.

"All right. I guess it's a plan then."

All of the kids are thrilled with the idea—even Mike looks excited for a split second until he sees me watching him. As soon as our eyes meet, his face settles back into its usual expression of bored intolerance. But it's too late. I saw it. For the tiniest fraction of a second, I saw an interested little boy in those eyes.

Just as Sean predicted, Arthur approached the boys with the same matter-of-fact manner as the pet store owner. He acted like he simply assumed they would behave in the same way as any other student would, and for the most part, they did.

"Check it out, Ms. S! I cut out his butt and back legs!" Donny holds up a curved piece of wood with a flourish.

"That's super." He nods in agreement and high-fives his volunteer, Jonathan, a student from the grade eight class who seems to really enjoy being with the boys. I hadn't thought about the idea of "reverse" integration as an option for my students before this. Bringing other students in as role models, and as a way for my guys to have connections out in the broader school population, might be a good way to start integrating them.

Every time I think about the whole integration question,

I start to sweat. My program's ultimate goal is to provide my boys with the academic and social skills to allow them to return full-time to a regular classroom—without anyone being punched, kicked, or sworn at in the process. I haven't figured out how we're going to do it with only two of us. I mean, I can't send any of them unaccompanied to a classroom, at least not yet. But if Sean goes too, then I'm left on my own.

Maybe that would be easier next year if I were closer to the office.

If I'm doing this next year. The jury is so far from in on that one.

"Hey, check out Kevin! He's like the jigsaw champion!" Cory is hopping up and down in excitement. Sean puts a hand on his shoulder to try to calm him a bit, which doesn't really work but at least keeps him in one spot. Kevin is standing at the jigsaw, with Arthur right at his elbow, and he's just burning that wood through the blade, twisting it when it needs to be twisted and turning it when it needs to be turned. It's amazing to watch. It's so much harder than it looks, as I can prove with my own slightly demented-looking reindeer, which I cut out first to demonstrate to the boys.

Mostly I demonstrated that I am not very crafty, much to their amusement. This time, Mike didn't even bother trying to hide that he was laughing too.

All seven reindeer were finished within our three-day window, and we retired them all back to the classroom for sanding and painting. This quickly became a favorite activity, one we could use to encourage—code for bribe—them to get their work done.

It became a favorite activity for Sean and me, too, not only because of the work aspect, but also because it seems to create a social atmosphere in the room. With their hands busy sanding and their eyes focused on the wood, the boys started having casual conversations with us and with each other.

"I really like skateboards. Do you like them, Donny?"

"Yeah. I used to have one, but it's at my mom's."

"That sucks. What about you, Kev? You like skateboards?"

"Skateboards suck!" Everyone laughs. Kevin tries out new phrases on a weekly basis. Last week everything was cool. This week everything sucks. Mostly we still have no idea what he really thinks about anything.

"I have a skateboard. At least I used to. My dad took it away when he was mad. But I totally rule!" My ears perk up. I've never heard Chris mention his father before.

"I never had a dad," Donny says. "Is it cool?"

"Everyone has a dad. You need one for sex or there aren't any babies! Didn't you know we all come from people screwing?" Chris laughs but doesn't answer the question. Donny flushes a little. I realize I should probably say something to Chris about his choice of subject matter, but I'm too interested in listening to them have an actual conversation.

"Yes, I know that! I just mean he bailed before I met him. I think it would be cool to have a dad instead of just a mom. Is your dad cool, Kevin?"

"Maybe. Maybe not." Kevin answers enigmatically to enthusiastic laughter.

"My dad's a deadbeat!" Cory chimes in loudly.

"What's that?" Chris asks.

"I don't know for sure, but my mom says that's what he is and that's why we have to move all the time. She says he's an asshole, too, so maybe deadbeat and asshole's the same thing." His voice is cheerful, and we don't bother interrupting to clean up his language. After all, he's really just quoting.

"Well, I don't care about dads. I just need my mom. Soon I'm going home. I'm going to give my mom this guy for Christmas." Donny is now convinced that his destination date for a full-time return to his home is December 25th. I have tried to reach his social worker to see what the reality is but haven't heard back. So mostly I just listen to him endlessly planning his reunion and try not to say much.

And so it goes. Chatting together about their unimaginable lives, giving Sean and me just the slightest glimpse of their realities.

We're sitting around sanding and chatting on a Friday afternoon when Mrs. Callahan makes a rare appearance at the door.

"I need to speak to you for a moment. Privately." She doesn't even look at the boys. I wish she would. They look awesome sitting there, working away, all calm and casual.

"What's up?" I ask as soon as we get a couple of steps down the hall. She looks at me solemnly. I get a sinking feeling in my gut. Is she going to break the brand new rules and tell me there's another kid starting in five minutes or something?

"I just had a call from Donny's social worker. There's been an accident. His mother is dead." She throws the words at me in three quick pitches.

"What?" My voice rises and tears instantly pop into my eyes. He's down there right now madly sanding a reindeer to

185

give her when he goes back home. It's all he talks about. How can she be dead?

"I didn't get details. Just that it was sudden. They want you to tell him."

"What?" This time I'm even louder. What is she talking about? I can't tell him his mother's dead! I don't know the right way to do that. That's his foster mom's job. Or his social worker. Or someone—anyone—other than me!

"She told me the foster mom doesn't feel she has a close enough connection with him to tell him on her own. He hasn't been there all that long. At this moment in time, you are the person he's been with the longest, so Children's Services would like him told here. His foster mom and social worker will come here, and you can all tell him together."

"And you agreed to this?" *Obviously.*

"I didn't really see where I had a choice. Besides, I think it's probably the kindest thing for him. He's really fond of you." She tries a small smile under somber eyes. I just shake my head.

This is a bad idea. This is not the right place for him to get this news. Nowhere would be the right place to get this news, but at school? It doesn't matter whether he's fond of me or not. I'm just his teacher. I shouldn't be telling him his mother is dead!

"Did anyone call Da...Mr. Norton? He is the psychological consultant. I think he needs to be here. He knows Donny. He'll know the right way to tell him."

"If you think it's necessary, I'll try to reach him. You just need to have a normal day down here, and then we'll keep him after school and tell him."

She walks away, but not before I see the quick flash of sympathy in her eyes. I'm not sure whether it's for me or Donny. Maybe it's both. I stand there for a second rubbing my aching eyes and trying not to cry. A *normal* day? He's in there painting that stupid reindeer, and I have to watch him do it, knowing what I know.

I'm going to call Daniel myself just so I know for sure that he's going to come. I need someone here. He's been coming around more since the accident, and the boys are actually starting to treat him like he belongs here. We have been hoping this would allow him to do some assessments later in the year.

I didn't think we would ever need his help for something like this.

I take a second to peek into the room where everything is still going well. Sean looks at me quizzically, and I just shake my head. I point down the hall and he nods. I run down to the phone and try the board office. Of course Daniel isn't there, but I leave an urgent message and then force myself to go back to the room.

The rest of the day passes in a blur. I break all the rules and let them work on the reindeer even without doing other academics first. It's unbearably painful to watch Donny, but at the same time I can't stand the thought of fighting with any of them today. I manage to get Sean aside long enough to tell him what's going on, and we both spend the rest of the day red-eyed and heavy hearted.

"Donny, your social worker is coming after school today, so you won't be going in the cab," I tell him gently at home time. His eyes light up.

"I bet she's taking me to my mom's! I had a good week, you know." He grins excitedly, and what's left of my heart breaks.

Sean gets the other boys off and then comes back. By the time he arrives, Donny's social worker and foster mom are here. Daniel arrives at about the same moment, and I close my eyes in relief.

"Hey, why are you here?" Donny asks him. Daniel just smiles and sits beside Donny. He takes one of Donny's hands in his and then he just does it. No prep. No fancy words. Just rip the bandage off and let the wound bleed out onto the floor.

"Donny, I have very sad news for you. Your mother has died." He gathers Donny close against his chest, as if trying to keep him from coming apart. Donny looks at him in disbelief for a second, but then seems to see something in his eyes.

"No! Mommy! Mommy!" He screams the word over and over and over as Daniel rocks him gently. After about thirty seconds, Daniel looks at me and gestures for me to take over. After all, I was supposed to be the one to break the news— and his spirit.

"I'm so sorry, Donny." I say the useless, empty words as I take him into my arms, rocking him back and forth in a pathetic facsimile of comfort. His grief is too painful for any of us to bear, filling the room until none of us can breathe.

His foster mother moves over, and we play pass the broken child. Daniel touches me on the arm and gestures for us to leave them alone. I don't want to stay. It's so terrible, I can't stand it. But I don't want to leave him either.

"They have to take over now," Daniel says to me quietly.

He gently ushers me out of the room where Sean is standing in the hall, openly crying and shaking his head. I give him a hug, and he holds on tightly for a couple of seconds.

"Poor little guy," Sean says, choking a little on his own sobs.

"I know." The tears start to pour uncontrollably, and the three of us move away from the door and the pain inside my room. We have to go home now, to our own lives, and try to put Donny somewhere into a compartment in our minds, where he will sit until work starts again next week.

I have to go home and try to be just a mom for the weekend. Try not to think about Donny. Try to erase the image of his cheerful grin as he painted *Mommy* on his reindeer. Try not to imagine what life would be like for my girls if something happened to me.

Try not to grieve for my little boy in front of my little girls.

CHAPTER 21

Smile

I didn't think it could get any worse, but—unbelievably—it does. On Monday I receive two requests.

First, Donny asked that I attend his mother's funeral on Wednesday. Mrs. Callahan said she could find someone to cover my class, but that I should try not to stay away too long because the other boys are likely to be upset.

As if I'm going to an afternoon tea party instead of the funeral of my student's mother, who died while he was living in foster care because I sent him home from school one day because I couldn't control my own students.

And now I'm taking the time to feel sorry for myself. Classy.

The second request took the shattered remnants of my teacher's heart and scattered them across the skies looking for somewhere else to be. Donny wants his wooden reindeer so he can give it to his mom after all. He wants it tucked into the coffin. He's been told that this will be done.

I walk into my classroom and pick up the stupid wooden deer. It's made out of four puzzle pieces of jigsawed wood, carefully fitted together so that it stands up and looks at you with vacant, black, painted-on eyes. Donny gave it a big red nose and a red smile as well. The words "To Mommy" are painted in bright blue across the side.

"Blue is my mom's favorite color," he told us.

The deer is staring at me.

"Stop smiling at me," I tell it. It doesn't listen. Maybe I should sic Baby on it. She'd wipe that smile off its face.

I carry it down to the office, where Mrs. Callahan said she'd hold it until someone came. I had offered to take it to the funeral, but they needed it there early. Apparently guests aren't supposed to shove things into the coffin. Or maybe it's because they're actually going to let Donny give it to his mother in her coffin. The thought makes my throat swell until it hurts so much that I can't swallow.

"I know this will be difficult for you. It matters, you know." Mrs. Callahan looks at me as she takes the reindeer into her custody. She looks at it for a second and then briefly closes her eyes.

"What?" Nothing really seems to matter right now.

"It matters that he cares enough to want you there. That he wants this for his mother. This place…you…matter to him."

"It's not enough, though. This is a school. He lost his home and now his mother. This place. It's just not enough." My voice breaks, and I feel a tear slipping down my cheek. I don't bother wiping it away. She rests her hand on my shoulder in a quick gesture of comfort. It doesn't work. I still really just want to hide under her desk and cry myself to sleep.

"It's something," she says gently, putting the reindeer on her desk, where he stands, looking obscenely festive, cheerfully guarding her office. I glower at him for a second and then turn and walk back to my class.

The boys are quiet after I tell them why Donny is away. Even Mike looks upset, perhaps imagining losing his own mother.

"Sucks," says Kevin, using the word correctly today.

"Totally sucks," agrees Cory.

The next couple of days in the classroom are relatively easy. No fistfights and few threats. Some work gets done. By Wednesday, I'm feeling like perhaps they'll all survive without me long enough for me to survive the funeral.

The chapel is about half full of people I've never seen before. Donny is nowhere to be seen, so I find a seat near the back. I'll give him a little wave when he comes in so he knows I'm here and then slip quietly out the back when it's over. That's my plan.

Five minutes later, the family comes in. Donny is walking between an older woman I don't recognize and his foster mother. I wonder if the first woman could be his grandmother. She's holding his hand as they stand solemnly looking at the coffin. I imagine the reindeer lying in there with Donny's mother. It makes me feel a little sick. I want this thing to start so it can end quickly.

"Ms. S! Ms. S!" The voice is piercingly loud and interrupts all of the hushed conversations. I look up, startled, and see Donny looking at me. He has a big grin plastered on his face and is waving madly at me. He whispers something to the older woman, who nods. Then he lets go of her hand and comes running back to me.

"I'm glad you came! Come and see my mom!" He grabs my hand and starts pulling me toward the front of the room. Every single person is staring at me, and I realize that refusing to grant a grieving child his wish at his mother's funeral will not go over well. I let him tug me up the aisle, trying not to trip and fall on anyone on the way up.

"She's here!" he says to the older woman. "This is my nana. Nana, this is Ms. S." She smiles at me with tired, lackluster eyes sunk in a careworn face.

"Nice to meet you. He's been looking for you. He can't stop talking about Ms. S." She doesn't smile again. Just shrugs and sighs. She looks at Donny with an expression that I can't read.

"Come and meet my mother," Donny says. I really, really don't want to do this, but I have no choice. He pulls me over to the open coffin and makes me look in. I know by now that his mother died of an overdose. No one knows whether it was an accidental one or not. I don't want to look at her and wonder if she left him on purpose. But I do.

The makeup people who do the impossible job of making dead people look...less dead, I guess, have made it appear that she is sleeping comfortably. She's a lot older looking than I expected, but maybe it isn't so much age as the life she's had.

"See! Look!" Donny reaches over as if to touch her. I involuntarily reach out, thinking I should stop him for some reason. He doesn't touch her, though. He just points to the top of the reindeer's antler that's peeking out by his mother's left shoulder.

"That's lovely, Donny." The words stick in my throat, and I have to cough so I don't choke on them.

"It's time to sit down now," one of the staff says gently, and we take our seats. I am now in the front row with the family—such as it is. The coffin is closed up, and Donny looks shell-shocked for a second, as if he has just realized that his mother is actually going to stay inside that big wooden box with that little wooden reindeer. He sits staring for a few more moments and then seems to shake it off.

"I can't come to school today. I have to go to the graveyard. I'll come tomorrow instead," he whispers to me as the service begins. I just nod at him and try to focus on the words flowing down from the pulpit. I don't actually register any of them.

I use the necessity of getting back to my class as my excuse not to follow the coffin to the next stage in the day. I say good-bye to Donny and his nana and head back to the school.

The boys are sitting at their desks, with Sean and Ms. J slipping from one to the other, helping them with what look to be word searches. I had left mostly "fun" activities for the day, figuring it might make life easier.

As I walk into the classroom, the first thing I see is a row of fully painted, ruthlessly happy reindeer grinning at me from the back of the room. I wish I had a large, heavy bowling ball right now. I'd send them right into the maw of the volcano.

"Hey, Ms. S. How's Donny?" Sean is watching me watch

the reindeer. I try a smile, but I can't manage it.

"He's...okay. Under the circumstances. I'm here now, Ms. J. Thanks so much for your help." She smiles at me, that slightly sad kind that doesn't really reach the eyes.

"No problem. The students were great."

"Nice to hear." I'm so tired that I feel like I'm going to fall down.

None of the boys ask me about Donny. No one says anything to me at all. They just keep on going about their business as if nothing is different here. As if no one has died.

"So, are you okay?" Sean asks, after the endless day finally ends.

"Of course. It wasn't my mother who died." I realize that the words came out harshly and try another smile to take some of the venom out. I still can't do it, and the poison lingers in the air, filling the classroom with its acrid fumes. Sean doesn't seem too adversely affected and just pats me on the arm, as if he's the mature one in the room and I'm the twenty-year-old.

"Go home and spend some time with those beautiful girls of yours. It'll make you feel better." I look at him and nod.

The pleased look in both daughters' eyes when I show up early starts to make me feel better. An early supper at our local greasy spoon, complete with chocolate milkshakes, lovely mounds of fries, and easy conversations about life in junior kindergarten versus life in grade three and the excitement of the upcoming holidays...and life starts to feel a little less bleak.

My life, anyway. I'm trying not to think about what Donny is doing right now.

This is going to be our first holiday season as a "chick" house. That's what my friend calls it now. She thinks that I should see my impending divorce as a liberating time in my life. I'm free to do what I want now—to raise my children as I see fit, to decorate my home the way I want to, listen to the music I want to listen to, eat whatever looks appealing to me.

Free to worry about money and custody and the emotional damage to my children. Free to wonder if I'm going to stay free forever. *Poor baby*.

Every night I sit down in the basement, hiding in the laundry room while I finish the girls' "big" gift. In my infinite lack of wisdom, I decided that I would make them something this year—because I'm not busy enough at work or being a single mom. And so I chose to make a Victorian dollhouse from a kit. I figured it wouldn't be all that difficult to do. After all, it's a kit, right?

I didn't bother to read the not-so-small print on the side of the box that said "professional level." I didn't look at the back of the box where the materials were listed. If I had, I might have seen words and numbers that would have given me pause for reflection—words like "1,000 cedar shakes."

One thousand teeny, tiny cedar shakes to be individually glued onto a roof that started out as a few pieces of wood that I had to cut and attach. Virtually everything in that box was raw material that required following intricate directions in order to make a five-bedroom house with about fifteen windows and three staircases.

I thought about taking it to school and getting Arthur to help me, but decided that I'm too stubborn for that. I've been working every night from the time the girls go to bed until about midnight, trying to get this miniature lumber pile to look like something that will make their eyes light up with excitement.

One night, I spent two hours trying to straighten out one of the stairs at the entrance way because I was afraid someone might trip trying to go into the house. The *doll* house.

Maybe I could have a tiny little house fire, collect the insurance, and buy them the new Barbie van instead.

I used to love the holidays. Even though it's mostly artificial, that whole deck-the-halls holiday spirit has always made the world seem a little shinier.

Maybe it's all the lights.

This year, I just want to get it over with so I can see that we all survived. I wonder what the holidays are like for my boys? I wonder what school will be like for all of us when they come back after two weeks of a completely different life. I don't imagine it's going to be cool, calm, and collected in our room in January.

I imagine Mike's stocking will be full to the brim with everything he has ever wanted. I'm sure Kevin's parents would want to fill his also, but I don't know if he talks enough even at home to tell anyone what he might want to see under the tree. A new whale maybe? Although we seldom hear from Baby anymore now that Kev is trying to do his own talking.

Cory's mother most likely has completely forgotten that there's a holiday coming up. If she does remember, all of the gifts will have either Bobby's or Alvin's name on them. Silly raccoon. I wonder if his head wound has stopped oozing yet or if she'll knit him a little hat for the winter. I've yet to see one on Cory's head.

And Chris? I still don't like to think about what goes on in that house on any day of the year, let alone at a time that comes with such high expectations. I wish he would say something that we could take to Children's Services so that something could be done about...whatever is going on. But he comes to school relatively well dressed, clean, and apparently well fed. No obvious signs of physical abuse. Only worries and suspicions about what he is witnessing, or worse, participating in, at home.

I know Donny won't be having the Christmas of his dreams. I don't even want to imagine what that day will be like for him. The loneliness he will feel without his mom.

Loneliness seems enhanced during those times when the media tells us we should be with family.

Most of the time I try not to notice that I'm alone once my babies go to bed or when they're with their father on Sunday afternoons. It's been a little easier lately, what with all of the house construction keeping me so busy. Add on endless thinking about school, and you have a mind and body with little space left for feeling lonely. At least that's what I tell myself.

But I do have to keep enough space in there to keep track of how my girls are doing with all of the changes they're going to be dealing with this holiday season. I have to hold it all together for them.

I have to try to keep my life separate from the lives of my students so that I don't accidentally self-destruct and turn into useless pieces of myself—a disassembled reindeer looking for his smile.

CHAPTER 22

Gone fishing

The first day back after the holidays is about as wild and crazy as I expected. Two weeks away from what passes as a routine in our room, and it feels as if we have started over at the beginning. Seemingly nonstop bouts of yelling, swearing, fighting, and endless meltdowns are keeping the time-out room busy virtually full-time.

I'm starting to think that I'm not the only one who spent the holidays riding an emotional roller coaster, flying uphill one moment and crashing down the next, until my stomach tied itself into so many knots that I couldn't get then undone in time to come back to school.

Everyone is basically nuts.

Except for Donny.

Donny came back acting as if nothing at all had

happened. He doesn't talk about going home to his mother's anymore, of course, but otherwise it seems to be business as usual. Actually, if anything, he seems a little calmer. There have been fewer physical outbursts, and he even seems able to ignore the other boys when they're trying to get him going, which is pretty much all the time. I can't help but wonder if in some strange way his mother's absence has changed his stress level. He isn't constantly worried about when his next visit is going to be or how long he has to wait until he moves home.

Then again, now he has to worry about where he's going to spend the rest of his childhood.

Before the break, Sean and I had been thinking that we were starting to get the hang of dealing with these guys. Not all of the time—not even close—but some of the time we felt like we were actually figuring out how to be proactive in helping the boys find ways to avoid conflict instead of always having to jump in to mitigate the damage after the fact. Our days were actually inching toward a routine. Friday would sometimes creep up on us, and we'd be pleasantly surprised to find out we had made it through a whole week instead of desperately trying to survive each day intact. We were both feeling like we might actually survive the whole year intact.

That feeling pretty much disappeared after three days of absolute chaos that almost brought both of us to the point of heading to the nearest bridge for a quick leap into the water. By day four, the tide appears to be turning, ever so gently, as life in our room starts to slow down. A few of the knots begin to come loose, and I have hope that maybe I can come to school without that anxious feeling in the pit of my stomach, wondering who is going to get smacked upside the head today.

Every once in a while I actually teach something curricular, like a math concept or some science. It's a challenge to figure out how to do that here. Although the boys are close in age, they come from three different grades at the moment. Combine that with endless days of missing classes and all sorts of learning issues that have yet to be formally identified, and you have quite the recipe for a convoluted set of lesson plans.

Most of the lessons are individualized, in an attempt to get each student from point A to wherever he needs to go. But I also try to do group lessons so that each of the boys gets experience in paying attention to someone who isn't necessarily talking directly to him. It becomes a combination of social skills and science or whatever other lofty curricular goal I set on a given day.

Everything in this classroom becomes a social-skills lesson, whether or not it starts out that way. The topics are endless. How to show people you're listening to them. How to show people you want them to listen to you. How to have a conversation. How to join a group already having a conversation. How to wait your turn. How to deal with teasing. How to stop teasing others. How to deal with someone yelling at you without punching or swearing. How to deal with someone ignoring you. How to ignore someone who is bothering you. How to deal with negative reinforcement. How to deal with positive reinforcement.

Come to think of it, maybe none of us should be taking these skills for granted. Most of us could use a refresher course in social interaction. The staff room springs to mind. If the kids only knew what goes on in there....

✗

"All teachers are asked to send a runner down to the office with Winter Activity selections by nine-thirty today. All permission forms must accompany the selection sheets." The announcement interrupts my lesson on the universe. Nothing like starting small. The boys are actually listening, and I resent the intercom enormously at times like this.

"You seriously mean that we're not at the bottom looking up? We're, like, in the middle?" Cory is totally fascinated by the idea that the earth is a sphere floating in space. Like explorers of old, he had the idea that the earth is flat.

"What's winter activity mean?" Donny asks, interrupting the already interrupted lesson.

That's a great question to which I don't have a great answer. I know the answer, but I don't know how to share it without upsetting everyone in the room.

Our school has a Winter Activity Day every February. It's a huge, complicated undertaking involving all sorts of field trips to local ski hills and skating rinks. Virtually the whole school is involved, with all of the grades mixed together, creating a nightmare of logistics for the teachers involved. The planning is extensive and begins the minute we get back in January. Permission forms are sent home right away, and there's a whole complex first-come first-served organizational horror that I've managed to stay out of since starting work here.

We were never given permission forms. I don't spend any time in the staff room anymore, and I didn't make it to the lunchtime activity meeting because I was down here with the boys, so I wasn't really paying attention to the fact that this school-wide activity day was being planned without us.

I know that it would be difficult for my guys to participate. Even though life is calming down in the classroom, they still have trouble with anything different or less structured, especially when large groups are involved. We've just recently started to try them outside for a few minutes during regular recess. Both Sean and I go out, and we've created restrictive physical boundaries. We follow them around like stalkers, making sure no one gets hurt. So far, it's been okay, but there've been enough close calls that we're still treading very carefully.

But it's like the prom. Even if you don't really want to go, it's nice to be asked.

And now I have to come up with something to tell them.

"We'll talk about that later. Right now, we have a science lesson to finish." *Typical teacher cop-out.*

"So what do you think? Can we come up with something to do?" I ask Sean later, after the kids are gone. I managed to put off the Winter Activity Day question just long enough that everyone forgot about it. Everyone but me.

"Well, I have kind of a weird idea."

"That should work. Everything we do around here is weird. What's your idea?"

"Well, I heard Sharon talking yesterday, and she was saying that the kindergarten kids aren't involved in the day either. Too young or whatever."

"I know. They usually do their own thing."

"Well, what if we get our guys to plan some activities for them? Here. We could invite them over to do stuff. Like a fishpond maybe. I used to love fishponds when I was little."

I look at him for a second, considering. Actually coming up with a way for them to do something positive for someone else? Sounds like something a teacher should have thought up.

"That's a really good idea. Not sure if Sharon would be comfortable bringing her kids over here, though."

"You could at least ask."

Good point. Maybe Sean should be running things around here.

It's such a wonderful idea that I'm almost afraid to ask, though. I don't want her to say no. It would be so lovely for those little kids across the hall to see us all as nice people instead of the monsters in the closet next door.

To my great surprise, Sharon is fine with the idea. She tells me that she's noticed the difference in my boys and the atmosphere in my room and that she thinks the idea would be good for everyone. I think we're growing on her.

Maybe I've been so worried about…everything, I guess, that I haven't fully registered the changes in my room. I've been trying so hard to protect everyone that I might be holding my students back from inching their way out into the real world again.

We decide that we'll ask volunteers, older kids who aren't participating in the winter fun for whatever reason and parents of the kindergarten kids, to bring small groups over to our room to check out the fishpond.

"A fishpond—like with fish?" is the first question when I share our brilliant idea with the boys the next day.

"Yes and no. There are fish, but usually they're made out of plastic or something. The children try to catch a fish, which is then exchanged for a prize. We will have to make the fish and the fishing poles and figure out what to use as prizes."

"Can we fish too? I want a prize." Chris always gets right to the point.

"Yeah, can we have prizes too?" Cory jumps straight up out of his seat, and Sean laughs as he puts a calming hand gently on his arm.

"Sure. We'll fish first to make sure it works. Does that sound okay?" Everyone nods or shouts his approval. I give Sean a thumbs-up, and he grins at the excitement his idea is already creating.

We spend part of every day for the next week creating our pond. I scrounged around inside the shed at home and found an old plastic wading pool. The boys cleaned it all up and covered the bottom and sides with blue construction paper, complete with awkwardly cut wave patterns to simulate water. We make piles of little paper fish in a rainbow of colors. Each fish has a small magnet glued to its nose.

"Do fish really have noses?" That question led to a rather lively lesson on fish and how they breathe.

Fishing rods are made out of lightweight bamboo sticks that I found at the dollar store. We carefully tie yellow string to each rod and attach a paperclip to the other end, practicing both fine-motor and frustration control at the same time.

I approached the manager of a local restaurant who was happy to donate a bag full of little giveaway toys that they hand out to their customers' kids.

Chris and Donny cooperated nicely in painting a big sign, which we mount proudly above our newly finished pond. And we're ready for business.

The day arrives with great excitement all round. The boys each have their turn, just to make sure everything works, of course. And then the moment of truth.

The first group of little people comes in, looking apprehensive. My guys stand there in stunned silence, looking even more apprehensive. The adults all smile encouragingly, trying *not* to look apprehensive.

"Hi! I'm Donny. Who wants to fish?" Donny breaks the silence, and suddenly everything is all right. The little ones all clamor to be first, and the boys start to smile as they hand out rods and show small hands how to find a fish.

Everyone is so focused on what they're doing that I actually find a few moments to sit back and enjoy the show. I can feel a big goofy smile taking over my face as I watch Mike carefully manipulating the string on a little boy's rod so that it attaches to the fish he's aiming for. Chris is digging through the toy pile, making sure the prize he picks is right for the pig-tailed princess looking at him with big trusting eyes. Kevin is busily throwing fish back into the pond and making sure that all the rods still have strings. Donny is the master of ceremonies, inviting each new group in with a flourish and directing the kids back out the door when they're done.

Cory is having a bit more trouble keeping it under control. He's bouncing around, trying to help, but most often getting in the way. But he's having a good time, and Sean is sticking close to make sure that doesn't change.

It's all so amazing—a moment of magic that will stick with me when we hit tough days ahead.

By the time we're done, twenty-five little people have caught a fish and taken home a prize. My guys are tired and proud of themselves, and we reward them with a video served up with popcorn.

Everyone goes home happy today.

Especially me.

CHAPTER 23

Saltwater tears

The euphoria created by the fishpond stayed at the back of my mind as a rosy-colored haze while life returned to its usual pattern of ups and downs.

One of the ups is that Sharon and her students all seem a little less afraid of my class now. Sharon pops her head in to say hello when she passes by, and her little ones actually say "hi" to my boys when they see them in the hall, instead of running away in terror.

A second up came in the form of another one of my spontaneous art lessons.

A few weeks before spring break, I suddenly got tired of looking at a large, menacing volcano every morning when I came into class. Even though it represented a brief moment of teamwork in an otherwise disjointed and chaotic first term, I decided it was time for it to go.

I grab some buckets from Mr. Z, along with a few old rags, and we all set to work scrubbing the wall. I expected lots of moaning and groaning from the boys, figuring that cleaning wasn't one of their favorite activities, but no one complains. Of course, we're doing this instead of math, which might have something to do with the unusually high level of compliance!

After about forty-five minutes of very, very messy scrubbing, we try to dry it with paper towels.

"Looks like someone shit all over the wall," Cory says to a chorus of giggles.

"Cory! Language!" I use a stern voice to mask my urge to join in the giggle fest. He's right. It does look like shit. The whole soap-in-the-paint trick doesn't seem to work when the paint is applied in such massive quantities. The previously cream-colored wall is now a dull brown, with liberal speckles and streaks of black and orange accenting it.

"I guess we have to clean it again," I say, this time to the moans and groans I was expecting earlier.

"This is too boring!" Chris whines.

"Sucks!" Kevin agrees.

"I know! Let's just paint over it. Something different this time!" Donny's suggestion is greeted with enthusiastic rumbles. Sean grins cheerfully at me, shaking his head. I have lost control of this situation—but in a good way, I think.

"Okay then. Go for it. But make sure the wall is good and dry first or anything you paint on it will look like...mud." I hesitate just long enough before the last word to make everyone laugh.

"Ha! You were going say sh—"

"Language, Cory!" Which just makes everyone laugh more.

Sean and I drag all of the paint cans out again and add soap, even though it likely won't make a difference this time either. I give them a veritable rainbow of options, hoping that the new design doesn't require quite so much brown and red. The boys huddle together at the wall, talking about their new creation.

"Sean, come here for a second." Donny calls out in a stage whisper that makes it clear I am not to be part of the conversation. Sean walks over, and they chat for a moment in hushed tones. He comes back over to me with a giant smile on his face.

"They would like you to wait out in the hall. They want it to be a surprise."

Ridiculously touched, I head out to the hall, where I stand within earshot. Their voices are loud and energetic, and their words are occasionally inappropriate, but they're having fun and working together so I stay out in willing exile until I receive my invitation to return.

"We're done, Ms. S!" Donny skips out into the hall and grabs my hand to tug me back in. Like any teacher/parent, I'm prepared to tell them it's wonderful, no matter what it actually looks like.

"It's wonderful!" The words come honestly and maybe a little tearfully. I can't believe how wonderful it really is! Instead of an angry and hostile volcanic eruption, there's an underwater scene, filled with shades of blue and green that brighten up the whole room. There are a couple of what seem to be man-eating sharks swimming about—after all, it is my class—but there don't seem to be any men actually being eaten. I can't see any dismembered body parts floating around. I do see that Baby is there, larger than life and leaping dramatically out of the water, the queen of the seas.

It doesn't take a psych degree to get the implications of the change in scenery.

On the other hand, they might just be riding on the high from the fishpond.

Either way, it's them, and it's great.

One of the downs that comes at me a few weeks later is the final step in my divorce process. All of the financial and emotional wrangling has boiled down to a few sterile-looking typed pages, the manuscript of my failed marriage just waiting for me to sign off on it. As my lawyer only works mornings, I have to make an appointment during school hours to get the signing done.

"Take the whole morning. You'll need a bit of time. Take the whole day if needed." Mrs. Callahan seems almost understanding. I start to wonder if maybe the "Mrs." is just for show.

"It won't even take the full morning. I'll be back before lunch," I say bravely and selflessly. I'm neither one. I just don't want to sit home alone feeling sorry for myself. I would rather work. My boys are good therapy. Nothing in my life seems quite so tough when I'm faced with their problems.

The appointment is short. I already know the story, so I read the words quickly. The document is filled with legalese that masks the reality of what it's really saying. I sign and initial in a dozen places and walk out carrying an envelope. It doesn't weigh much, but it's unbearably heavy in my hand.

I throw the envelope into the trunk of my car and drive back to the school. As I'm pulling into the parking lot, I'm surprised to see a police car pulling out. Did Mike decide to kick his cab driver's seat again? Did Callahan make good on her threat? I look at it closely as it slowly passes me, and my surprise turns to shock when I see a small face pressed against the glass staring at me. I slam on my brakes and get out of my car, somehow thinking I can stop the cruiser from getting away. It keeps on going, and I see Cory again, this time just his eyes as he tries to see me out the back window.

I park quickly and run into the school, straight to Mrs. Callahan's office. As I walk in, I can hear her on the phone.

"So, I know you're having a hard enough day. If you don't feel you can come in and deal with this, please just stay home. I'll fill you in tomorrow." She looks up when I barge in without an invitation.

"Oh, I was just leaving you a message!" She points to the phone.

"What's going on?" I'm still standing, Cory's eyes burning into my brain.

"Sit down, and I'll explain."

"I'll stand thanks." I need to be ready to run. Whatever happened is serious, and my other guys will be upset.

"Cory has had a rough morning. He came in very agitated. Sean feels he hadn't had his medications, but we were unable to reach his mother to confirm that."

"She never answers. I asked her to get his prescription changed so we could give it to him at school, but she never did it," I explain, even though Mrs. Callahan's expression clearly states that she isn't looking for explanations.

"Anyway, he couldn't calm down and then he had an altercation with another student, Michael, I believe. Sean was down the hall with yet another student, and Mrs. Miller was unable to control the situation."

"Mrs. Miller? Where was Ms. J?"

"We decided that Ms. Jackson needed to be with her own students today. That it was time to try a supply teacher with your class." She looks at me for a second as we both process just how bad that decision was.

"The situation escalated, and Cory was taken down to the time-out room when Sean returned. He was so upset that Sean couldn't be in the room with him at first. And then he destroyed it."

"What?"

"The room. He destroyed the room. He tore the couch apart. Actually pulled the paneling from the walls. He just couldn't stop. So we called the police."

Now she calls them. Not when Chris was running down the side of the highway to another town.

"I should have been here. I could have calmed him down. I should have tried to make the stupid appointment for another time." I rub my eyes, forcing back the tears that are trying to fill them. Crying is not the right response here.

"You couldn't have known this would happen. Your class has been so much calmer recently. Besides, you have to take care of yourself sometimes, too." Her voice is soft, even kind, and it makes me feel even more weepy. I don't trust myself to speak, so she takes another turn.

"This is a tough situation, but it's just the reality with these kids sometimes. We can't help them all." Her tone is still gentle, but the words are starting to scare me.

"What do you mean? This is only a single incident. We can still help him." I look at her quickly, ignoring the saltwater starting to leak down my face.

"No. I'm sorry. He's out. His mother will have to find something else for him. His behavior was simply beyond extreme. I can't risk the safety of my other students." Her voice sharpens, as she stabs me with her decision.

"No, that isn't fair. If I had been here, it wouldn't have happened. We can't punish him for that!"

"This is a school, a community. He has to be able to function with or without you. I am responsible for everyone here. This is my call, and it's final."

I look at her, shaking my head. This is the woman who told Mike's parents that we don't ever suspend students. And now she's expelling one. It doesn't make sense, and I look around inside my addled brain, trying to find the words to tell her that in a way that will turn this all around.

I look at her for a second, and she stares back calmly. Decisively. Nothing I say right now will change her mind. So I don't even try. I just turn around and leave, scrubbing at my face as I storm down the hall so that the boys won't see any traces of my useless tears.

The class is quiet when I get there. No one is talking; no one is out of his seat. Everyone looks like he's doing something work-related. Just a regular class of hard-working boys. Sean looks up when I walk in. His eyes say it all.

"Sorry," he says quietly. I shake my head.

"It's not your fault. It's no one's fault."

The first part is true. The second is a flat-out lie. There's fault here.

My fault. I should have made the lawyer schedule a time that was convenient for me. For Cory. I should have checked that Mrs. Callahan had done the supply-teacher bit correctly.

Mrs. Callahan's fault. She should have told me she wasn't using Ms. J. I wouldn't have gone. She shouldn't have called the police. She shouldn't have decided that he's gone forever without talking to me or to Daniel.

Cory's mother's fault for caring more about a raccoon than her kid.

Mike's fault for being so nasty to the other boys all of the time.

The system's fault for not giving either kid's family the help that they need.

Blame it on everyone.

Blame it on no one.

He's still in a police car heading for nowhere.

Mrs. Miller, the supply teacher, is looking at me. She looks like she really wishes she hadn't answered the phone yesterday. I try a polite smile in her general direction. It hurts my face.

"I'm sorry you had a rough time. I…well, I wish I had been able to prepare you a bit. Anyway, if you don't mind, I'd like to go down the hall for a second or two and then I'll be back and you can go."

"That's fine." She tries to smile.

I walk down the hall and stop outside the time-out room. I close my eyes for a second and then make myself open the door. It looks like a small army of expert vandals went to town in here. The couch is turned upside down, the pillows thrown across the room. One of them is ripped open, and the stuffing is spilling out onto the floor. He must have ripped it open with one of the jagged pieces of wood created when he somehow managed to pry the siding off the wall with his bare hands. He's pulled it down in several places, breaking it in the process, leaving splintered pieces all over the floor.

I reach up and try to pull a loose board off the wall. It's nailed on securely, and it takes two hands and all of my strength to get it off. How much rage must this little boy have inside him to be able to create such havoc?

So many broken pieces everywhere. How will he ever get fixed?

And now he's just gone. We have no say at all. He just has to start over. Not that we made any huge strides with him. We didn't make any miracles. We didn't cure him.

But he's ours. Part of us. We care about him.

That doesn't matter. We "can't risk the safety of our other students."

What about Cory's safety?

I close the door gently and head back to class. I stand at the doorway for a moment, staring at the peaceful ocean view and wishing I could just jump in and sink down to the bottom, so I could shut out the world and let my tears for Cory blend with the saltwater until everything is washed away. Instead, I walk into the room and thank Mrs. Miller for her help; she scurries away quickly, likely never to be seen again.

"Hey, Ms. S, how was your appointment?" Donny asks me. I look at him a bit startled. I'd almost forgotten why I was gone.

"It was fine. Thanks for asking." Always thank someone for asking how you are. Social lesson number—*oh, who cares?*

"Cory freaked out. Cops came." Our classroom has the unfortunate distinction of being right beside the parking lot, so there's always far too much to look at. This time they definitely saw too much.

"Fucking cops," Kevin adds. Mike snickers. I whirl around, angry that he'd find anything funny in this moment. I open my mouth, ready to say something about how guilty he is in all of this. He just stares at me with big, blue, innocent-looking eyes.

He's nine years old. Whatever he's said and done, he's only a kid. If I'm going to talk to him, I can't do it from anger. I have to be older than he is.

So right now, I'm not going to talk to him. I'm too mad. Besides, he likely doesn't even remember what he said to Cory.

"Kevin. Please don't use that word," I say instead. Kevin looks at me. I'm pretty sure he doesn't know which of the two words I don't want him to use.

"Let's just get back to work, everyone," I say, falling back on teacher speak to get us through the afternoon. I really hope no one decides to have a blow between now and home time. I don't have a time-out room anymore.

At the moment, I feel like I could use some time out.

From everything.

CHAPTER 24

The bullies and the bullied

"So, did you have any luck?"

"No, she's not taking any calls at all. She left one message a few days ago that basically said she was pulling him from our jurisdiction. Well, not in so many words, but that was the gist. She said a few other things, too, but I don't think you need to hear them."

"Maybe I do need to hear them. Maybe I need to really understand how colossally I screwed this up." I slump down into a chair. It's about a week and a half after the Cory debacle, and I've been trying to reach his mother pretty much every day. I just want to know how he's doing, where he is. But there's no answer, so I asked Daniel to try, thinking Cory's mother might be more responsive to someone more official.

"You didn't screw anything up. You had a personal

appointment. That's allowed, you know. You couldn't have anticipated this happening." He sounds reasonable, but I'm not buying it. I'm not in the market for reasonable right now.

"It's not even about this one incident. It's that after several months of being in my so-called special program, he's still so out of control that this could happen.... I haven't done one thing to change him in all that time. What's the point to all of this if I can't help them?"

"You are helping them. Even without proper resources or physical space or staffing, you're still making a difference."

Yeah, right. They're all cured and will go off into the light to live happy, productive lives. "I don't see that at all. Not one of them could walk into a regular class and survive for more than a minute. One wrong word from someone in the room would set them off, and all hell would break loose."

"That's probably true," he agrees. "They aren't ready for that yet. The classrooms they'll be going to need to be ready, too. None of that is in place."

"What do you mean?"

"There's work to be done on both ends if integration is going to work. Your guys are used to being bullies, controlling everyone and everything through loud voices and lots of fighting. But they're also used to being bullied by different people in their lives. They're the misfits that other kids will pick on. Not just kids either. They come with reputations that put everyone who deals with them on edge. Your students need skills that will help them deal with kids and adults getting in their faces. The classes they'll be going to need skills in pretty much the same things."

"I think most classes need that, whether my guys are

coming their way or not."

"Absolutely. But you just need to focus on the ones that will affect you. Like I've told you before, pick your battles. Just like you do every day in class."

"Yeah, well, there are lots of battles to pick from." I shake my head. I don't even want to be having this conversation. The last thing I need to think about right now is integration. I can't even control them here. How can I keep them from being total class bullies anywhere they go?

"Don't forget that there are lots of good moments too. That's what you have to hold on to. It's hard to learn that as a teacher. I used to work in a school on a psych ward. My kids could eat yours for breakfast and spit them out at lunch. Most days I didn't think I managed to teach anything to anyone. It was just survival."

"And how did you survive?"

"I figured out that the only thing I could really do is give them one good moment at a time. And if I was lucky, the moments added up to an hour—sometimes even a day. I couldn't cure anyone. All I could do was accept them and try to teach them what I could fit into those moments."

It all sounds so wise and wonderful. Like something out of a heartwarming TV movie where the super fantastic teacher puts all of her desperately broken students back together again, all in two hours minus commercial breaks.

"What if there aren't any good moments?" My class is a whole different kind of show.

"You have to look for them. Like Kevin starting to say something other than 'dickhead' and leaving his whale at home."

"Yeah, well, you can thank the half-ton truck for that one."

He raises his eyebrows and smiles a little. "I think it's probably more than that. Although the truck helped. What about Donny?"

"Donny? You mean the kid who I got taken away from his mother so that he never ever lived with her again?"

He shakes his head at me without smiling this time. I know I'm being obnoxious, but I can't seem to help myself.

"You know that's not really true. And maybe you saved him from being there when his mother overdosed." He's trying a little too hard to be positive.

"That's a stretch."

"Maybe. But you gave him a safe place to find out about her death. He had someone he trusted in his life. He wanted you at her funeral because he felt like you cared about him."

"It's not enough though."

"Sometimes it's all you have to give them. And it's enough in that moment." His voice is persuasive, but I'm not in the mood to be persuaded.

"It just seems...so little. I need a psychiatrist."

"For them or you?"

"Ha ha. Probably both. But I need someone here to figure them out and fix them so that I can teach them. Like at the Section school."

"Psychiatrists aren't magicians either. It's all a process. There are so many reasons these kids end up the way they do that no one 'fix' is enough."

"So what does it take? How do we stop them from being bullies and stop everyone else from bullying them at the same

221

time? I don't think the whole one-moment-at-a-time thing is enough. I want to know how we cure them!" *Now I'm being loud* and *obnoxious. I think I'm spending too much time with my boys.*

"In a perfect world, they wouldn't need curing in the first place. In our not-so-perfect world, the problem is finding a system where all of the adults in their lives have the resources and time to work together to figure out how to give them a chance. To get governments to give us enough money so we can put intervention programs in place so that we're catching issues early and not having to try to put kids back together with Band-Aids later on."

"So how do we make all of that happen?"

"If I could find the easy answer to that, I'd write a book and make a million dollars." He sighs a little and shrugs his shoulders. I want to keep on arguing about this until he gives me an answer I can live with, but I can tell by his face that it's not going to happen.

"Anyway, I will keep trying to find out more about Cory, but in the meantime, I have some news that you aren't going to love."

"Oh?" My voice squeaks a bit. He laughs.

"Yeah, the superintendent has decided that you need to fill in the empty space with a new student. Sorry."

"That's okay. I figured it would happen soon enough. Well, not quite this soon, but we'll manage."

So now we just forget about Cory and grab the next broken kid we can find. If the bandage doesn't stick, just move on to the next patient.

"We have a meeting with Mrs. Callahan after school. I'm

headed over to the other school now to get as much info as I can. The principal is supposed to come back with me, but don't hold your breath on that one."

"Okay. Thanks for letting me know. I guess."

He gives me a small apologetic smile and heads off. I close my eyes for a second and take a couple of deep breaths. A new student. Just what we need.

It's been so nice the past two weeks. That sounds awful... as if I'm glad Cory is gone. I'm not. I feel sick about it. But it's definitely quieter without him. He's a constantly moving force in our room, and without his frenetic energy, it's been easier to see the forest for the trees with the other students.

That will end with the arrival of a new one. Change is never fun for my class, and in our room nothing is worse than someone new to figure out and compete with and make fun of and try to set off. Someone who might be smarter or tougher than they are and who will make fun of them and manage to set them off.

My boys. The bullies and the bullied.

Just like everyone else.

Just like me, sitting here, being completely negative about a child I know nothing about. Exactly the attitude I worry my students will face when they go back to regular school. I would guess that the poor new kid will be less than thrilled to find out he has to come here. The last thing he needs is to feel that I don't want him in my class.

Daniel arrives back at the school at lunch time, and we're sitting in Callahan's office.

"So, he has been in a regular class, but spent most of his time in Resource. Typical scenario. His principal said they were managing him until the latest incident." Daniel looks down at his notes, which he had to bring instead of the other principal—as predicted.

"Which was?" Mrs. Callahan looks up at him.

"Well, he decided to run away. Or roll away is more accurate, because he was wearing rollerblades. The principal followed him in his car and managed to get him to come back to the school. At which point, Justin kicked the principal in the leg with his roller blades still on and took off again. And now he's on his way here."

"Still wearing the rollerblades?" I ask. Daniel laughs. Callahan does not.

"Is that the extent of the violence?" she asks, glaring at me.

"No. Lots of fights. Threats. He has a history of illegal drug use, which fuels some of his issues, I think."

"Drugs? I have no experience with that. My boys are too young!" We have enough issues with their legal drugs. My knowledge of the illegal kind is pretty much limited to what I learned in high school health class, combined with TV commercials and the occasional news story.

"Well, unfortunately, that's not really true. Your boys just haven't gone that route. At least not that we know of. But Justin is older. Twelve, I think. He's in a group home now where the drug problem is being addressed. It shouldn't be an issue at school, I don't think." He looks uncomfortable. His eyes keep shifting away from mine. That isn't a good sign.

"Do you think he's a good fit for the class?" I say it slowly and distinctly, stretching it out a bit because I don't really want the answer. It's fairly obvious what it's going to be.

He looks down for a second and then sighs a little and looks right at me. "No. Not really. He's older, bigger, and more street-smart. He'll be a problem. Especially for Mike, who thinks he's the tough guy in the bunch. And Donny, who thinks he's the class leader. I expressed my concerns to the superintendent, but he said we don't really have a choice. There's nothing more restrictive that's available to him right now, and you have space."

Great. My little group across from the kindergarten crew is the most restrictive option right now, so he just comes here whether it's the right thing or not?

✗

When he arrives Monday, Justin is pretty much as advertised. Taller than me, but thankfully still shorter than Sean. A wise-beyond-his-years look in his eyes and a permanent sneer on his lips don't inspire much confidence. He's twelve going on seventeen, and the other guys see it.

"Justin, this is Donny. And Kevin. And Mike. And Chris." I point to each student as I introduce them.

"Whatever." He doesn't look at anyone. Just takes the seat that Sean points out to him and looks down at the desk. The other guys look at each other and then over at him. No one says a word, not even Mike.

They just know.

For the next little while, we all tiptoe around in a charged atmosphere. It's so strange—even stranger than usual. Everyone gives Justin a wide berth, and he pays absolutely no attention to anyone. He makes a half-hearted attempt to do the work I put in front of him and tunes out completely during class lessons. During recess, he just stands against a wall, watching.

No one talks to him. Ever. I keep waiting for Mike to try him on for size, or Donny to try to be friendly, but there's nothing. Just this...feeling that something isn't right.

The bullies and the bullied.

Can't imagine anyone bullying this kid.

CHAPTER 25

Exit route

"Do you think it's okay to take Justin?"

It's about two weeks into our strange new existence. We've spent every day carefully tiptoeing around on eggshells, trying not to break any. Justin is still just watching, and the others are doing their best to pretend he isn't there. Mostly all we do is watch him watching us. I should be thrilled that I have such an "easy" new student, but it all just feels...creepy. That's a terrible word to use about a kid. But he is creepy. He just stares. His eyes kind of bore into you like he's looking inside for weak spots to exploit at some later date.

That song keeps running through my head...*Every breath you take, every move you make, I'll be watching you.* Stalker song.

Paranoia adds so much to the quality of my teaching.

The school track-and-field day is coming up, and we have

actually been invited to attend, which created a set of mixed emotions made up of about two parts pleasure and at least four parts sheer terror. Most of the class has never been to a track meet before. They were usually in whatever group was left behind at their schools due to having committed some infraction or another. So we started preparing right away and have been working hard for a while now, practicing both the actual activities and the proper reactions, should those activities fall apart at the seams. As in, try not to punch anyone in the head if you don't win the race. And don't laugh in anyone's face if you do win the race. The whole "it doesn't matter if you win or lose, it's how you play the game" concept is pretty out there as far as my guys are concerned. Their lives have been a constant struggle, each of them fiercely determined to win every battle just to survive in a world where they don't really fit in. Casualties are part of the package, and none of my boys spend too much time worrying about who gets hurt along the way. It's every kid for himself. The concept of fair play doesn't really enter into it.

Grace under pressure. It's hard to teach them how to deal with an artificially designed competition when every aspect of their lives is a real one.

We have extra volunteers coming so that we're at a one-to-one ratio. We've talked about it over and over. We've role-played every scenario Sean and I can come up with. We've visited the field over at the high school so that we're used to the environment and ready to give it a try.

Everyone is excited. It's a pretty big test of the next phase of their school lives. A return to trying to be a part of things in the larger school.

But Justin is such an unknown quantity that I'm afraid to take him. He hasn't participated in any way in our prep sessions, other than to stand and stare, of course, arms folded across his chest, occasionally shaking his head in what I assume is disgust.

I'm surprised he and Mike haven't become firm friends. They could bond over their overwhelming disgust with everything I do.

"There's nowhere else for him to be. I can't ask the group home to keep him just because of a track meet. You are a special program after all," Mrs. C says. I try not to growl.

"Could we at least ask that one of their trained workers come along?"

"Sean works in a group home, doesn't he? Just make sure he's with Justin."

It's not the same. First of all, Sean is terrific with the kids, but he isn't actually a fully trained child and youth worker. I think we need someone with the right training to deal with whatever issues are lurking beneath Justin's too-calm exterior. Besides, I want someone with Justin who knows him. Someone who can predict him and maybe even control him if he ever loses it. I don't bother to say this out loud, though. She's made up her mind, and now all I can do is hope for the best.

✗

Track day dawns with clear skies, crisp, cool air, and a slightly nervous group of boys.

"Don't like running," Kevin announces the minute he climbs out of his cab.

"You don't have to run, Kevin. Remember what we said? It's enough to just come and watch." We aren't going to push it. Attendance is mandatory, but full participation? Not so much.

"Don't like watching," he growls.

"It's okay, Kev. You can just watch me. Then we'll just hang out, okay? You like hanging out with me, right?" Donny comes up from behind him and taps him on the shoulder. Kevin doesn't like to be touched but tolerates it from Donny. He tolerates most things from Donny. They're as close to friends as anyone has been in our room. Donny shows a gentleness when he's with Kevin that makes me wonder who he would have been if his life had been kinder. Who he will be if life gets kinder.

"Okay." Kevin nods, and the two of them head into the school with Sean.

Mike and Chris arrive next, and I send them in, knowing they'll only be a few steps behind the others. I'm pleased to see that Mike is here. He proclaimed track day to be stupid when he left yesterday and vowed that he would force his parents to keep him home. I don't know if he changed his mind or if he couldn't change theirs. Either way works for me.

I wait for Justin. His cab arrives, and I stay where I'm standing. He gets out slowly and stands on the curb for a few seconds, pretending he doesn't see me. He hates the fact that he has to be escorted into the school every day "like some kind of little kid." He's wearing heavy jeans and combat boots, I assume because we asked the kids to wear track pants and running shoes for the day. He stands for a few more seconds, as if waiting to see what I will do. Or maybe he just doesn't want to get moving yet. Either way, I decide to stay where I am, waiting to see what he will do.

It feels a bit like we're having one of those childish staring matches, where each of us is trying to make the other one blink. I really hope he blinks first. I think I need to win this one.

After a few more seconds that feel like minutes, he shakes his head and stomps past me into the school, being very careful not to look at me at all. I follow directly behind him, trying not to stomp but treading loudly enough that he knows I'm here. He keeps stomping until he gets into the classroom and sits down. The others ignore him, as usual.

"Is everyone ready?" I ask redundantly. They look pretty ready to me. Everyone but Justin has track pants and running shoes on, as requested. They even have sun hats and water bottles.

"Okay, well, as soon as announcements are over and our volunteers get here, we're off to the races." I smile at my own great wit. Sean laughs. Everyone else just groans.

"Don't like races!" Kevin practically shouts it.

"It's okay, bud. You don't have to do any racing unless you want to." Donny pats him on the back. Kevin just shrugs his shoulders and growls a little. I can see Baby peeking out of his backpack, which is a testament to the level of his nerves. She's been staying home recently, letting Kevin do his talking completely on his own, but it seems he needs some moral support today that we lower-level species just aren't equipped to give him.

We head off to the field about ten minutes later, Sean sticking close to Justin without getting right in his face. Chris, Kevin, and Donny all have eighth-grade students walking with them. Chris and Donny both seem to really like the idea and are chattering away at their new "buddies." Kevin is muttering to himself, probably about how much he hates track and field. I assigned myself to Mike, who is less than totally pleased with the arrangement. He won't look at me or talk to me. But he's here. And he has running shoes on. And a hat. Which is a pretty high level of compliance for Mike.

We arranged things so that we could all be at each activity to cheer the boys on. I wasn't sure if anyone would actually go through with an activity, so I'm really excited to see Donny head right over to the long-jump pit.

"Watch this, Ms. S!" He takes his turn and actually manages a pretty good jump. Chris gives him a high five as he comes back over to join us.

"Cool. It's my turn now. One hundred meters, right?" Chris looks at Sean, who checks the schedule he's carrying and nods.

"Yep. Starts in five minutes. Let's get over there."

We all troop over to the track. Unsurprisingly, Chris picked all running events. He didn't even need to train.

"Kevin, you're signed up for this one too," I say gently. We arrive in time to see other students start to line up. I feel a swell of pride watching Chris head over on his own, as if he's done this a hundred times before.

Kevin looks at me and then looks at the kids lined up waiting for the start signal. I smile at him, fully expecting a loud, gruff "no."

"Okay," he says, to our astonishment.

"Good for you, Kev!" Sean says.

"Awesome, Kev!" Donny agrees. Mike and Justin say nothing. They're both carefully trying to look like they don't belong with us...or each other.

Kevin goes up and stands beside Chris. We chose the hundred for him because it's short. Kevin is the kind of kid who spends a lot more time watching TV than running around outside. I don't imagine he does much exercise in any given day, other than what I make him do at school. None of that matters now. I'm just thrilled to see him there in the lineup with all the others.

"On your marks, get set...GO!" The voice cracks with excitement as the kids sprint forward.

Well, most of the kids sprint forward.

"Wrong way, Kev! Turn around!" Sean calls out, choking on his laughter while he tries to get over and send Kevin the other way. Kevin ignores him and runs about ten meters in the opposite direction of the other runners. Then he stops and looks at us.

"Racing sucks."

"You're awesome, dude!" Donny laughs and runs over to Kevin, grabbing his hand and forcing him to do a high five.

We're all laughing so hard we miss the fact that Chris managed to come second in his heat. Luckily, his volunteer is more on the ball than we are and is standing at the finish line to congratulate him.

The rest of the morning goes remarkably well. Mike actually does the four hundred that he signed up for and seems cautiously proud when he manages to finish in the top five.

Donny runs in the two hundred and gives the high jump a shot. He seems unconcerned that he didn't place in either. Kevin's brief career as a track star ended at the backward ten-meter line.

By lunchtime, we're all feeling pretty good about ourselves and the day. Except for Justin, who spent the morning glowering.

"Okay, everyone. We're going to head over to the far side of the field and sit down and have some lunch." I start walking, all of the boys trailing behind me. We come to a large chain-link fence, and Sean accidentally starts walking on the other side. The kids all laugh at him walking along beside us, but separated by the wire.

"You look like you're in jail or something," Chris says.

"What do you know about fucking jail!" Justin yells at him, speaking for the first time all morning. Chris looks at him, startled.

"Fuck you, asshole! I'm just kidding around!" Chris yells back. Justin looks at him for a second and then, before anyone realizes what's happened, he leaps on him and throws him to the ground. He starts pummeling Chris with his fists.

"Stay back!" I yell at the other kids as I try to get hold of him to pull him off.

"Look out!" I look up at the sound of Sean's voice. He's on the top of the fence, somehow managing to clear it in less than a second. He comes flying down on our side and lands beside Justin, grabbing him and flipping him off Chris all in one fluid motion.

"Cool!" I hear Donny's voice behind me.

Justin goes into full freak-out mode, screaming and struggling as Sean tries to get him into a safe enough hold to calm him down. Chris has scrambled away and looks like he's ready to fly.

"Chris. I need you to stay with us. This isn't your problem anymore. Let Sean deal with Justin so you can go back to your day." I don't want to sound like I'm pleading. Even though I am.

"Hey, Chris. Come on man. Stand here with me. We still have to eat lunch and do your second heat. It's okay." Chris's volunteer, Greg, steps over and puts a hand on his shoulder. I give him a shaky smile of thanks.

"I need you all to stand over by the fence until we get Justin sorted out," I say to them. Sean has him held tightly now, but Justin isn't calming down. He's yelling and screaming and drawing attention from other students and parents.

"Someone get this bastard off me. He's hurting me!" Justin has noticed that he's drawing an audience and is trying to play to the crowd.

"What's going on here?" A woman is standing beside me, watching curiously.

"Please, I need you to move away. We're dealing with a situation here." I sound like a badly directed TV cop. The woman moves a few feet away but keeps watching. Justin is still yelling about how much he's being hurt, and it's still drawing attention.

"Please! I need you all to move away. This young man is having a difficult time, and all of the attention is making it worse!" I finally raise my voice. Another teacher from the school has joined the crowd, and I ask her to find Mrs.

Callahan and tell her to meet us in the parking lot. I know she has her car here, and I'm going to need help getting Justin back to the school.

Justin finally starts to slow down. I don't know if that's due to the lack of an audience or just because he's getting tired. Either way, he slumps to the ground, lying still.

"All right. I'm done. Get off me, faggot!" he says to Sean. Mike snickers. He looks like he wishes he were Justin right now. There's definitely admiration in his gaze.

"I'll get off when you're actually done—which means finding another way to talk to me," Sean says calmly, holding on tightly but without pressure.

"Okay. I'm done. I'd like to get up."

Sean slowly gets to his feet, bringing Justin up along with him. He keeps one hand clamped around Justin's arm.

"You can let go," Justin says, wiggling his arm.

"No, I don't think so," Sean says as he basically frog marches him down toward the parking lot, where I'm relieved to see Mrs. Callahan is waiting beside her car.

"I am not impressed, young man!" she says to Justin when we reach her. Justin doesn't look impressed either.

"I'll come in the car with you and Justin," I say to Mrs. C. "Sean and the volunteers can walk back, if that's okay."

"We can't stay?" Donny asks, looking totally disappointed.

"I'm sorry. There isn't another teacher here to watch you. It's just not safe."

"Not fair either!"

"No, it's not. Anyway, you guys can have activity time in the classroom after lunch. By the time we get there and have lunch, there'll only be about an hour left anyway. It's the best

I can do." I shrug my shoulders and get in the backseat of the car with Justin, who has retreated into disgusted silence.

When we arrive at the school, Mrs. Callahan tells me to put Justin into the VP's office while she calls the group home.

"Is he all right there on his own?" Ms. Keller is still over at the field with the rest of the kids.

"He seems pretty docile right now. I'll just be a minute. You go and get your class settled and come back up here when you're done."

I head off down the hall. The boys are in our room, eating their lunches. No one seems all that upset anymore. Donny and Kevin are charmingly demonstrating the contents of their mouths to each other, while Chris talks with Greg. Sean is sitting with Mike, who actually seems to be having a conversation with him.

"We've decided on a video for the afternoon. Okay with you?" Sean looks at me. We try not to overdo the video thing so it can be a treat. All of my whirling dervishes seem to be able to sit quite nicely for movies, and the temptation to show one every day is pretty overwhelming at times. Today is definitely the day for it.

Once the food is gone and the movie is running, I head back to the office. Callahan informs me that the group home staff have been called and someone is on the way.

"I have to head back over to the track. There's been an injury and I need to bring the student back here. You'll have to stay with Justin until someone comes. Is Sean all right down there?"

"Should be. The grade eights are still with him. Sharon is across the hall because the little kids aren't at track. The cabs will be here in less than an hour, so there shouldn't be a problem. I hope." The one advantage to our program is that our day ends earlier than the rest of the school's by about an hour. This is mostly a distance issue, but it also works out well as a tolerance issue. Mine and theirs.

"Well, I should only be a few minutes. I guess we can bend the rules this one time."

If only she knew!

Mrs. Callahan leaves, and I go to the VP's office to see Justin. He shouldn't have been left alone, even if it was only for a minute. It took a lot less than that for this whole mess to start in the first place. I stand in the doorway for a moment looking at him.

"I'm sorry things turned out this way. Do you want to talk about it?" It's pretty obvious to me that Chris's simple comment couldn't possibly have been enough to upset him so much. There has to be a whole lot more going on here. He was just looking for a reason.

"No." He doesn't even look at me. He's sitting on a chair on the other side of a large teacher's desk that almost fills the very small room. I come in and walk behind him to lean casually against the wall, silently letting him know that I'm ready and willing to listen. He stares sullenly at the top of the desk, silently making it clear that he doesn't care. I stand in my corner, wondering what to do next. I have a fleeting memory of someone saying something to me about exactly this scenario. About how I should be standing somewhere else.

The thought leaves me before it's finished forming.

"Okay. Well, I assume Mrs. Callahan told you that someone is coming to pick you up."

He looks up, staring directly into my eyes for the first time ever. He has very intense green eyes—very intense *angry* green eyes.

"What!" The word shoots out and hits me between the eyes. I try not to flinch at the raw power of his anger.

"Someone from the group home is coming. You can't go in the cab after a violent incident so close to the end of the day. It was part of our agreement when you first came here." I keep my voice calm and cool. The director of Justin's group home had requested this. He told us that once Justin gets upset, he stays that way for a long time, keeping himself at full throttle, ready to take off again without notice.

"No fucking way. That kid had it coming. Talking about jail like he knows what it is. Yelling at me. No one yells at me. I'll get in shit if they have to come for me. I already have two strikes from that retard director. Jesus fucking Christ, what the fuck is wrong with you? Call them and tell them I'm going in the cab! You are such a retarded bitch, just like everyone else. Every stupid, fucking school is the same place full of assholes. Call the group home! Now!" He stands up as the words spew from his mouth—more words than he's used the entire time he's been here—swirling around us in an angry torrent. The dam he's meticulously constructed since coming here has come crashing down, and all the pent up emotion that he kept so carefully hidden breaks loose. My back is literally up against the wall, and I have no choice but to stand my ground.

"I can't do that. They're already on the way."

He looks at me and then down at the chair he just vacated. Before I fully register what's happening, he's grabbed the heavy metal chair and is swinging it in my direction. I instinctively raise my arms up over my face, and the chair crashes down on my left forearm. He's between me and the door, so there's nowhere for me to go. Ignoring the throbbing pain in my arm, I grab the chair so that he can't hit me with it again.

"I need assistance!" I yell, hoping I don't sound as panicked as I feel. I can't get around him to get out of the room. I can't let go of the chair or he'll hit me again, and this time he might have better luck getting my head. We're locked in a desperate tug of war, and I'm terrified that one of us is going to get seriously hurt.

"I need assistance!" I call out again. Justin just grunts with the effort of pulling the chair away from me. I try to maneuver our bodies so that I can get between him and the door, but he's too strong for me. I can feel my hands sweating, and I'm afraid I'm going to lose my grip on the chair.

"Hey—enough!" A pair of hands comes from behind Justin, grabbing him expertly, hugging both his arms against his chest until he lets go of the chair. Justin starts to struggle.

"I said enough!" The voice is strong, authoritative, and unafraid. It's the director of Justin's group home, a big man with a soft spot for children, who obviously knows his way around restraining kids. He looks at me.

"Are you all right?"

I resist the urge to hold my aching arm. It hurts almost as much as my wounded pride.

"Yes."

"You should always make sure you're the one with the exit route," he says as he backs Justin out of the room.

I nod slightly and watch them both leave.

I screwed everything up. My arm hurts like hell. And I'm still holding the stupid chair.

I definitely need an exit route.

Out of more than just this room.

CHAPTER 26

Aftershocks

I take the girls out for supper on the way home from daycare. They're both thrilled at the unexpected treat, and for a few minutes I forget my aching arm and how it got that way.

An evening spent with baths and hair washes and bedtime stories helps my memory fog over a bit more, and by the time the moon has come out to dominate the sky, I'm starting to feel almost human again. I pick up the TV remote and flip through the channels to see if there's anything on that will make the fog completely erase the day.

I'm idly flipping through without actually registering anything when the doorbell rings. It startles me in that unpleasant, instant panic, phone-call-at-two-in-the-morning kind of way. I don't get a lot of company. Our neighborhood isn't one of the friendlier places on earth, especially since

I became a single instead of a double. It's not like we had neighborhood block parties before the divorce, but at least people seemed civil enough. But for some reason, no one really seems to notice me at all now that I'm just me.

I head to the door, which is dead-bolted and chained. New additions purchased out of my anxiety at being here alone with two girls to protect.

"Hello? It's just me—Keith." A man's voice comes through the steel reinforced door panels.

Keith? I have to think for a minute. Oh. Keith. Of course. My "down the street" neighbor, who also happens to teach seventh-grade at our school. We don't talk much, at home or at work, so I can't imagine why he would be here. I really don't want to start talking to him today of all days. I'm not feeling very sociable. I open the door anyway because I'm pretty sure he knows I'm here.

"Hello. Is everything all right?" *That was a stupid question.* I can't imagine why he would come *here* if he had a problem.

"I was about to ask you the same thing. I heard about the incident today at school. I was telling Mary about it, and she suggested I bring you these." He kind of shoves a bouquet of lilacs wrapped in wet paper towels at me. The water drips down onto my feet.

"Oh, thanks. Thank Mary also." I don't know who Mary is. I guess it's his wife.

"And this. Figured you could use it after what happened. I make it myself," he smiles proudly as he hands over a bottle of what seems to be white wine.

"Thanks again." I stand for a moment, wondering what I'm supposed to do now. Closing the door in his face would seem rude to him. Standing here any longer seems rude to me.

"So, how's the arm? It's your arm that you hurt, right?" A quick bolt of pain shoots through it as if my bruise can tell that someone is talking about it.

"It's fine. The doctor said it's just a bruise."

"Well, I don't know how you handle those nutbar kids. They all should be locked away in my opinion." He looks at me as if expecting agreement. I can't be bothered to argue with him. Besides, right now, I'm not sure he's wrong.

"Well, thanks again," I repeat, gently starting to move the door closed in the universal signal for "please leave now." He looks like he would like to stay and share some wine and do some kid bashing, but I move the door again, and he gets the idea.

"Okay then. Just call if you need anything," he says, then heads off home to Mary.

I'm not much of a drinker, especially now that I'm home alone with the girls. Can't risk being unable to drive if there's some kind of crisis. But they're both sound asleep, and my arm is still talking to me. I think it's saying, "One drink won't hurt." Although, seeing as Keith made this himself, one drink *might* hurt.

I dig through the drawer for several minutes trying to find a corkscrew before realizing that the top screws off. I'm looking for a wine glass when the phone interrupts me. "Hello?"

"Hi, sorry to bother you so late. It's Daniel Norton."

Daniel? Why would he be calling? What disaster has struck now?

"Oh. Hi." My voice obviously sounds less than thrilled, and he laughs a little.

"I just got my guys to bed and wanted to check in on you."

"Your guys?"

"My sons. I think they're close to the ages of your daughters."

"Oh. I didn't know you had kids." Which is not surprising seeing as I only recently started remembering his first name.

"So, how's your arm? Did you see a doctor?" he asks, changing the subject back to me.

"Yes. Callahan insisted. Serious Incident Report and all that. The doctor said it's a deep bruise, but nothing's broken. He said I should ice it, take a painkiller, and consider changing jobs." I try a little laugh, but it comes out like a cough.

"I'm sorry this happened. I feel a bit responsible."

"Why? You didn't hit me with a chair."

"No. But I should have fought harder to keep Justin out of your room. I knew he wasn't a good fit."

"That's one way to put it."

"Yeah, well, he's not coming back anyway. His attack on you was very calculated and extremely dangerous. I spoke to both Superintendent Stewart and to the group-home staff and made it clear that he's a danger to himself and others— outside of the acceptable level, even for your class."

"It's my fault, too. I know better than to back myself into a corner."

"Doesn't matter. His behavior was still extreme, regardless of where you decided to stand."

"So where does he go now?"

"We are trying to get home schooling in place until

he can be in a Section placement. This isn't the first time he's attacked staff members at school and the group home. Between the drug issues and the nature of his violent episodes, we should be able to make a case. He needs the help that Section can give him."

"Most of my guys do."

"I guess that could make Justin the lucky one."

"That's one way to look at it. A really strange way." I shake my head, which has started to pound out harsh drumbeats of pain. A loud sigh escapes into the phone as I put my hand on my forehead and try to rub the day away.

"Are you all right?" I know he isn't talking about my arm this time. Or my head.

"I don't know. You told me to hang on to the moments. I didn't even have a moment with this one. There was nothing. We did nothing at all."

"I know. It happens. Some kids are just too far away for us to help them at school. Justin needs something different."

"Why is he like this? What happened to him to make him this way?" I know there isn't an answer. At least not a simple one. But I still feel like I have to ask.

"He's like many of them. A combination of who he is and what has happened to him. His dad's in jail, mother's an addict. He ended up in care. Which is kind of a funny word for it. He's smart enough to understand that his life sucks and manipulative enough to try to control it, even when he can't, which really, really pisses him off. And he's probably just as hurt as your other guys but not able to show it and work it through without someone getting seriously hurt. Complicated."

"Nature and nurture. And a whole load of other crap mixed in."

"Pretty much. So, anyway. Justin isn't coming back, and no one else will be filling in the space."

"Really? They figure I can't handle it?" My defenses fly up into the phone.

"No. With only a few weeks left in the year, there was an agreement that we need to wait until next year to add students. Once the classroom is moved, a proper time-out room in place, and proper staffing, the numbers will be looked at again."

"Proper staffing? You mean someone other than me?" For a second I feel something close to disappointment. *They don't want me back?*

Not that I necessarily want to come back. I mean, I don't want to come back. This year has been too crazy. Nine months later and I still don't really know what I'm doing most of the time. It's just like having a baby. Except my girls were stuck with me. No proper staffing option there.

"No. We're looking at the possibility of an extra part-time assistant to help with integration. Everyone is assuming *you* will still be there. Will you be?"

"That's a good question. I don't have a good answer though. It's been a hard year. And it's not even over. We still have to survive June. That's hard even in a regular class." *Whine, whine…*

Wine! I need to get this top off and pour a glass of wine.

"Well, I hope you give it some thought. You've done a great job with the boys who are still here. They've all come a long way."

247

"Even Mike?" *Who still scares the crap out of me sometimes. Although he's never tried to beat me with a chair. I guess it's all relative.*

"Absolutely. He participated in track and field without killing anyone. He stayed out of the whole Justin mess. It's progress. You just have to look closely."

"I'll have to start carrying a magnifying glass. You can call me Sherlock. Searching for clues that I've done something useful." *I have to stop whining and start drinking.*

"I have to go. You relax and take care of your arm. Will you stay home tomorrow?"

"No way. I don't need another disaster. They'll be better off with me there."

"I completely agree." I imagine he smiles as he traps me into ending on a positive note.

I pour some wine into my glass. It looks like real wine. I take a sip. It doesn't taste like any wine I've ever had, but I drink it anyway. Maybe it will help me make a decision about next year. If I decide I don't want to take the class again, I will have to tell Callahan soon. I don't imagine it will be all that easy to find someone else who's actually willing and able to do this job.

I wander upstairs and check on the girls, wine glass in hand like some kind of mother you'd see on TV. They're both sound asleep, snoring softly in that ridiculously sweet way that only children can.

Three more weeks until summer and then I get to be a full-time mom. I can't wait! Except for two weeks in July when they're going to have their first vacation with their dad. Without their mom.

Am I going to be able to handle watching my babies drive away for two-week vacations alone with their dad? Will they miss me? Will he remember to brush their hair and floss their teeth and read them a bedtime story? Was he paying attention when he was still here? Does he know what foods they like and what allergies they have? Does he know them?

Will they be all right away from me? Will I be all right away from them—two weeks sitting here all alone without even work to occupy me? I don't think I want to build another doll house, although the one I gave them for Christmas was a huge hit and still sits proudly in the middle of the living room floor.

I look around their semi-dark rooms. Haven't decorated in here for a couple of years. Maybe I should take the two weeks and completely redo their rooms as a surprise. A little paint and a little wallpaper, some new posters and maybe new bed covers—this would make a completely new world for both of them. I can be as wild and crazy as I want with no one here to tell me to do it differently.

This is going to be great!

I run downstairs, grab a pencil and paper, and sit down at the kitchen table. I start by listing ideas and materials, even trying a sketch or two, ignoring the reality that I am pretty close to the world's worst artist even when my arm isn't battered and bruised. Although right now it isn't hurting as much as it did earlier. It's actually feeling much better.

My forgotten wineglass sits there watching me.

It's still half full.

CHAPTER 27

Climbing downhill

Once June hits, most teachers see the rest of the year as a downhill slide straight into summer. Students definitely see it that way, so keeping control of a classroom can be a challenge at the best of times. We teachers plan all kinds of trips and special activities, both to pass the time and to use as either bribes or threats, depending on how you choose to look at it.

Bribes and threats don't work very well with my students. They live in the moment, in the truest sense, with virtually no thought given to any potential consequences of either words or deeds. You can promise them the world on the condition of one good day, and it won't really make much of a difference to how that day is going to turn out. They just don't have enough control over their internal or external lives to be influenced by the whole delayed-reinforcement deal—positive or negative.

What seems to work best is to try to get inside their moment-to-moment lives with them and try to help them deal with each individual triumph or defeat before moving forward. It's been hard to find the triumphs over the last couple of weeks. The boys are all totally on edge. They're basically taking turns freaking out over what looks like nothing much to Sean or me. It's starting to feel like the whole year has just disappeared, and we've completely circled back to day one.

We aren't slipping and sliding down any hill. We're clawing our way, climbing backwards, right to where we all began.

Even Kevin ended up paying his first visit to the time-out room, sobbing hysterically because we called him Kevin instead of Rainbow Rooster, or something equally odd. The fact that none of us even knew that he had transformed into a rooster overnight didn't seem to matter.

Chris managed to break his leg one weekend and came into school with a cast that reaches from his ankle right up to the top of his thigh. Of course, there was a plausible explanation that we couldn't challenge. Much as we felt sorry for him, we secretly agreed that, if he had to break his leg, this was the best time. It would slow him down enough that at least for the rest of this year we wouldn't have to worry about him running away.

Two days later, he decides that no cast is going to stop him.

"I hate math. It's too hard. I hate this place. I'm done!" He struggles to his feet and limps awkwardly to the door. Sean saunters over to him, knowing there isn't really any urgency to trying to stop him. After all, what's he going to do?

"Come on, bud. Let's sit down and talk about this," Sean says reasonably, as he and Chris reach the door simultaneously.

"Fuck you!" Chris shouts, and takes off down the hall, trying his very best to run.

"Seriously, dude?" Sean calls after him, shaking his head and trying not to laugh. He beckons to me to come over to the door. I walk over, followed closely by the other three boys. We all crowd the doorway, watching in fascination as Chris does a strange, weighed-down hop, skip, and run down the hall.

"He's pretty fast," Donny says, laughing.

"He's an idiot," Mike says, shaking his head.

"Fast idiot," agrees Kevin, which makes even Mike laugh. We watch him for a few more seconds, giving him a reasonable head start before Sean makes his way down the hall to bring him back to us again.

And so it goes. The panic bubble in the pit of my stomach is back as I come in each day wondering who is going to blow his top first. It's just nuts, and I can't seem to get it under control. I feel like calling Daniel and asking his advice, but he'll just tell me to live in the moment. Which I'm already doing. But most of our moments these days are hard ones.

This isn't making my decision about next year any easier. I'm flipping back and forth constantly, which isn't helpful to me or to Mrs. Callahan, who has been remarkably patient.

I can't think about next year when I can't even find my way out of this one without everyone around me exploding into tiny little pieces of themselves. There won't be anyone left to make up a class next year at this rate.

We might have to put that volcano back up on the wall. The whole peaceful underwater theme doesn't really apply at the moment.

✗

It isn't until the second-to-last week of school, with only seven days left, that I finally figure out what is going on.

Well, not so much figure it out as have someone tell me.

"What is going on with you? You haven't had a blow in weeks, and now this is the third one in two days!" I'm sitting with Donny in the time-out room. He's just had a full-out screaming, yelling, kicking, punching, wrestling match with Mike, which he seems to have started and which Sean finally managed to end. He's at the crying stage now, tears running quietly down his face as he sits at the table in the rather oddly decorated room, where the only concession made to Cory's rampage was to remove the fractured wood pieces from the floor and to put the couch back without its pillows.

"I have to do it. To stay."

"Do what? Stay where?" He looks up at me as if he thinks I might be stupid. Which is probably accurate.

"Be *bad*. Stay *here*." He enunciates carefully, just in case I still don't get it.

"You have to be bad to stay here? Because summer is coming? You can't be at school in the summer." He looks at me as if he now knows for a fact that I'm stupid.

"I know! It's just…this is a class for bad kids, right? I have to be bad so I can come back here. With you. I don't want a new school. A new teacher. Every year I have to go some-where else. I want to come back here." He looks at me, a shy little smile peeking through the tears. I feel my own eyes start to tear up a bit. I probably should be taking issue with his description of our class, reminding him that I don't believe there are "bad" kids. But this isn't the time for it.

"Oh, Donny. You don't have to do this to get back into my class. We still have lots of work to do together. It's okay. I'm sure you'll be able to come back here in the fall." As the words slip out of my mouth, I realize my mistake, but it's too late to do anything about it.

I'm not sure of anything. I can't tell him where he'll be in the fall. He could switch foster homes three times over the summer and end up so far away that I'll never see him again. I don't want to lie.

But it's finally penetrated my thick skull. Much of the crazy behavior is coming from fear. The uncertainty. Wondering what their summers are going to be like without the structure of school. Wondering what September will hold. Will they come back to something—someone—familiar, or will they have to start all over again…and again…and again…

Poor little guys.

I guess I am sure of something after all.

In this moment, I'm sure that I do have to be here in September. Just in case they find their way back.

Donny's revelation didn't stop the problems in our class, but it did help me understand a little better, which has allowed Sean and me to do an improved job of de-escalating. I might be overly optimistic, but things do seem to be settling down.

I hope so. I'd like to get to the end without another serious incident messing everything up.

"So, I have decided that I would like to do a last-day-of-school trip," I announce to Mrs. Callahan two days before the end of the year.

"This is rather short notice." She doesn't even look up from her paperwork.

"I know. But it's a very low-key trip. I'd like to take them to my place. My backyard, to be exact. I have a nice climber that's big enough for them to try, and I can put on the sprinkler or fill the wading pool, which isn't quite big enough but better than nothing." I'm talking quickly and a little too loudly. She finally looks up, and the expression on her face is one of complete incomprehension, as if I somehow slipped into a foreign language in the middle of my plea.

"Your home? You want them at your home? I don't think that's a good idea. There are all kinds of liability issues and…" Her voice fades away with the shaking of her head.

"Well, I actually checked it out with Daniel Norton. He said he can clear it with the board office and get us special release forms. I just have to increase my insurance coverage for that day…kind of like when you have to transport kids in your car. And Daniel even offered to come with us so that the ratio is pretty much one-to-one and so that we'll have a vehicle."

"How will you get there?" She's still shaking her head. She's going to get motion sickness. I know I'm feeling a bit queasy.

"Walking. It's only a few blocks. Daniel is going to pick up Chris because of his cast."

"What about your neighbors? How will they feel about you bringing…" She raises both hands as if she's lifting up air.

"Children to our hallowed streets? I think they'll be fine. It's none of their collective business anyway." Besides, I'm not telling anyone. Although I'd kind of like to see Keith's face when he finds out there will be nutbars on the street—besides me, that is.

"But I still don't understand why you waited so long to ask me about this. Why didn't you decide this sooner so you could have used it as an incentive. It could have made life easier."

"No. I don't want them to have to earn it. They need some things in their lives that simply *are*. I want to do this for them just because." I know she has no idea what I am talking about, but I smile sweetly at her anyway. It used to work on my mother.

"Okay. It's your…decision." She was going to say funeral. I'm sure of it. The thought makes me smile even more widely.

"Oh, speaking of decisions. I've made mine. I'm in for next year."

I leave before she can answer. I have a lot to do before the end of the day. Daniel and I decided to keep this to ourselves. He's going to call all of the parents and swear them to secrecy. The boys won't know until they arrive tomorrow. That way there won't be any extra pressure on them today to be "good," which inevitably leads to someone—or lots of someones—being "bad."

Not that we should ever, ever tell children they are bad—just that their behavior is. I read that somewhere. I wonder if maybe bad behavior should be labeled a little differently also.

Maybe we should do away with the word *bad* completely, unless we're talking about food or television.

CHAPTER 28

Time out

"Ms. S, check me out. I can see everyone else's backyard from here." Donny is standing at the top of the slide in my backyard.

"That's great. If you see anyone, just wave and shout Hello!" I call over to him from my deck, where I'm lounging comfortably on a lawn chair.

"Oh, okay! Hello! Hello!" he shouts loudly, endearing himself forever to my usually quiet neighborhood.

"Look at me swing, Ms. S. If I hold my leg straight out, I can go all the way!"

"I think you have to hold it straight with that cast on!" Sean laughs as he gives Chris a push.

"This was a nice idea," Daniel says, sitting down on the top step.

"Yeah, they're doing great."

"It's more than that. This is your home, and you have them here. Whether they can put words to it or not, it means something to them."

"Speaking of putting words to things…" I point to Kevin, who seems to be singing as he splashes away in my ridiculously small wading pool. I can't make out the words. I'm not sure they're even English, but there's definitely some sort of tune going on. Or maybe he's just crowing. Roosters do that.

"Even Mike is getting into things." Daniel points to the other side of the yard, where Mike is busily constructing a massive sand castle. I would never have pegged him for a kid who likes to make sand models, but then again, I know almost nothing about that side of him—the child underneath the "behavior" kid.

I sit here in my own backyard, wondering at the ease with which my two worlds have just collided, watching these boys simply being children for a moment in time. And it's a good moment. One to hold on to over the summer when I start wondering why on earth I promised to go back.

I wonder about their summers.

According to Kevin's mother, he has spent most of his summers inside watching TV. Will he take some of his new-found skills and go outside and maybe play with another kid? Will Baby stay inside and let Kevin do the talking?

Is Mike still chasing his parents around with kitchen knives, or have they figured out a place to hide them? Should I tell them to get him a sandbox so he has something more constructive to do?

Will Chris start running again when he gets his cast off? Will he run so far that we won't see him again in the fall?

Will Donny get to stay in his newest foster home until September? He seems to like this one. Does that matter to the people who make decisions? Will I see him again in the fall?

Will I see any of them?

I shake the future away and bring myself back into the present. Right now, it's a really pleasant place to be.

It's an awesome final day, and it makes the good-byes at going-home time both easier and tougher at the same time.

"Bye Ms. S! Have a good summer!" Chris calls out as he hops over to his cab. Sean helps him get settled in and gives him a high five.

"Bye," says Mike, somewhat curtly. But he looks at me for just a second, and there it is—that tiny little flicker of childhood that I so want to work on next year.

"Dickhead," growls Kevin, with just the slightest hint of a grin. Sean and Donny and I all laugh.

"Right back at you!" I ruffle his hair as he climbs into the cab.

Donny's cab comes last, and he heads over without a word. He doesn't even look back. When he gets to the door, he opens it and pauses. He turns and runs back over to me, grabbing me in bear hug.

"Thanks for helping me, Ms. S," he says quickly as he lets go and runs over to his cab.

I watch his car drive off and feel the tears welling up again. I am getting extremely weepy in my old age. Sean looks at me and grins.

"Hey, it's okay. I'm pretty sure they'll be back. And even

if they aren't, there are lots more where they came from! Have good one. Hopefully see you in September!"

"You too. I really hope you're around again next year. Take care of yourself."

He strolls off. I stay still, listening to the silence and watching the empty spaces.

Part of me just wants to call the cabs back instead of sending the boys off to uncertain futures that I might not be a part of. The rest of me knows that we all need a break, a little time out from school and from each other.

September will come soon enough, and it will all start again. My behavior boys will be back.

The bullies and the bullied.

If we figure out how to do it right, maybe someday—somehow—they won't have to be either one.

They can just be kids.

EPILOGUE

And in the end...

They did all come back that next fall, along with three new boys who arrived with their own unique set of challenges to help stir up an already very full pot. Sean found a job in another city, so the boys and I had to train someone new. We also got a new classroom and—most exciting of all—a new time-out room that didn't have tiny little children listening on the other side of the door.

My own girls survived their time away from me and were impressed with their re-invented rooms—rooms that changed every summer for the next five years or so. It took me a while to figure out how to occupy my time while they were gone. My youngest eventually stopped biting people, which was good, and stopped flying away at night with her glow bugs, which was kind of sad. I rather miss Chloe.

I haven't always been able to follow the lives of my students after they leave me. I know that Kevin found his way into a life-skills program at the high school after three years of splitting his time between my class and the "regular" class. He became quite the little talker, and I heard that he even got a part-time job at a local store after finishing school. Donny ended up living in one of the group homes run by the same man who saved me from Justin that day. The home had a therapist who formed a strong working relationship with Donny, much to our delight. Donny also stayed with us for three years, over which time he gradually made a successful return to full-time in a regular classroom, with resource support, before moving to a school closer to the group home. I hope life stayed stable for him. Mike came back for one more year and then disappeared from our radar. I heard a rumor that his parents decided to move to another area to get a fresh start. I hope they learned to hide all of their sharp objects.

I never heard a thing about Cory again—or his raccoon.

Chris stayed with us for two years. We had continuous concerns about what was going on at home but never had enough proof to back up our suspicions. We could only sit and worry after he left us to return to his community school, without any real supports in place. We couldn't persuade anyone to consider a more restrictive school setting, because he wasn't having enough in the way of "overt behavior issues" at school. His psych evaluation never happened. I think his parents canceled it, but I'll never know for sure. We all knew that something was horribly wrong, but he was too smart to let anyone in. Basically he was just cut loose. Released on his own recognizance.

Five years after he left us, I received a phone call from his mother. She called to tell me that Chris was living in a "lock down" group home awaiting his trial on charges of child molestation. I had heard of the case on the news, of the local teen charged with assaulting a number of young children, but hadn't connected it to any of my former students. It made me physically ill to think about Chris being the one in the middle of the horror story.

His mother told me that Chris was feeling worthless. Useless. He wanted to hear from someone who might still have some positive feelings about him. Someone who didn't think of him as a monster.

He wanted a letter from me.

Worthless and useless. So many of my students over the years have struggled with feeling that way. It's pretty hard to keep going when you don't think that anyone truly values you. It's a lot easier to kick and scream and prove to everyone that you are exactly what they think you are.

In the end, we all need to feel like we're worth something to someone, anyone.

We all need to feel needed.

It broke my heart to think that after five years, I was the only person he could think of to reach out to. Of course I agreed to write the letter, but honestly, I have no real memory of the words I managed to dredge up. I don't imagine I found anything to say that could have made even the slightest difference to the pain he must have been feeling.

So much pain. Pain that Chris most likely both witnessed and suffered all his life. Pain that he passed on to other children when it became too much for him to bear. Pain that those children and their parents will now have to deal with. Pain that his mother will carry with her forever. I have always felt that Chris was one of the kids that we lost. We didn't—couldn't—help him. He just didn't fit into the mold that was being used to shape the students eligible for help at the time that he needed it.

So often it feels like we don't give our most fragile children even a fraction of what they need. There is so much that still needs to be done to create and sustain the intricate connections between home, school, and the communities in which we live so that all of our children are given the best chance of survival in an increasingly complex world.

It *can* be done. The experts know what to do. But it will require a combination of global understanding, a significant pledge of financial support, and a true commitment to long-term change. The adults with the power to alter people's lives need to take some time out from all of their other important pursuits to remember the children.

In the meantime, I think about what Daniel told me back in that first wild and crazy year—that sometimes, all we have to offer are moments in time when life is a little less difficult than it was the moment before. Perhaps if we add enough of those moments together, we can help to create a safe passageway for all of our children through a world that doesn't always remember they're here.

It's not enough—nowhere close—but it might plant in them a tiny seed of hope that they are worth something to someone. To me.

ACKNOWLEDGMENTS

As always, I want to thank the wonderful staff at Second Story Press for their continued belief in me as an author.

I also want to acknowledge DG and MB, who are the pieces who made up the real "Sean." I could not have survived without the incredible support of the educational assistants who gave so much to our students.

Thanks to all of the teachers over the years who integrated my students into their classrooms in an attempt to help them find their way back into their home schools.

Always and forever thanks to my amazing girls, who constantly gave me a touchstone of sanity to come home to.

And of course, I have to acknowledge all of my wonderfully complicated and challenging students over the years, who, as corny as it may sound, always taught me more than I did them.

ABOUT THE AUTHOR

LIANE SHAW is the author of three novels for teens: *thinandbeautiful.com*, *Fostergirls*, and *The Color of Silence*. This is her first work of nonfiction. Liane was an educator for more than twenty years, both in the classroom and as a special education resource teacher. She spent several years working with students with behavioral and emotional issues in both school and alternative settings. She was later hired by her local school board as a consultant to help teachers and principals deal with students with special challenges. Now retired from teaching, Liane lives with her family in the Ottawa Valley.

She enjoys hearing from her readers, so feel free to write her at lianeshaw2014@outlook.com or send her a comment on her website, www.lianeshaw.com.